Kabbalah Concepts
Introductory and advanced concepts of the Kabbalah

Rabbi Raphael Afilalo

From the same author

The Kabbalah of the Ari Z'al, according to the Ramhal
Kabbalah Editions

Kabbalah Dictionary
Kabbalah Editions

Kabbalah Glossary
Kabbalah Editions

Kabbalists and their works
Kabbalah Editions

160 Questions on the Kabbalah
Kabbalah Editions

Kabbalah concepts
Kabbalah Editions

Kabbalah Editions, 2006 www.kabbalaheditons.com
www.ravraphael.com
www.ramhal.org
www.kabbalah5.com
rav@kabbalah5.com
ravraphael@yahoo.com

Publisher's Cataloging-in-Publication
Afilalo, Raphael
      Kabbalah Concepts: Introductory and advanced concepts of the
                        Kabbalah
 / Raphael Afilalo
p.cm.
Includes bibliographical references and index.
ISBN 2-923241-118 (Soft cover)
1. Cabala. 2. Mysticism—Judaism. I. Afilalo, Raphael. II. Title.
BM525. BM723 2005
296.1'6   2005938110

To my wife Simona

Approbations

MORDECHAI ELIAHU

FORMER CHIEF RABBI OF ISRAEL & RISHON LEZION

ב"ה

מרדכי אליהו

הראשון לציון והרב הראשי לישראל לשעבר

APPROBATION

[handwritten Hebrew text]

RABBI DAVID HANANIA PINTO

Rehov Bayit Vegan 57
Jerusalem • Israel
Tel: (972-2) 643 3695
Fax: (972-2) 641 2045 • 643 3570

בע"ה יום חמישי לסד "וישב" תשס"ז

שלום וברכה

המלצה

באתי באות להמליץ על הספר
"Kabalah Dictionary" (מילון הקבלה) שכתב הרב רפאל אפללו שליט"א בספר חז"ל
יש הגדרות ומונחים על קבלת הרמח"ל זיע"א הכל מסודר
בצורה נאה תועלת ללימוד ולעיון בו.

לאור ההמלצות חרבות שקיבל הספר, נשאר לי רק להמליץ
עליו בכל לב.

אני מברך בזכות אבותי הקדושים זיע"א את המחבר שליט"א
לברכה והצלחה ושיזכה להוציא מתחת ידיו עוד ספרים לזכות
הרבים ושיזכה מעלה מעלה בתורה ובראת שמים. אמן

ע"ה דוד חנניה פינטו ס"ט

[signature]

דוד חנניה פינטו
רחוב בית וגן 57
ירושלים • ישראל

כ"ק האדמו"ר
רבי חיים פינטו זיע"א
בנשיאות עיה
דוד חנניה פינטו
בן הרה"ג המקובל
רם משה אהרן
פינטו זיע"א

ישיבת בני חיים
כולל אברת חיים ומשה
כולל משכן בצלאל

רחוב בית וגן 57
ירושלים • ישראל

ORH HAÏM VÉMOCHÉ
11, Rue Du Plateau
75019 Paris • France
Tel: (33-1) 42 08 25 40
Fax: (33-1) 42 08 58 85

YÉCHIVA PINTO
20 Bis, Rue Des Mûriers
69100 Villeurbanne
France
Tel: (33-4) 78 03 89 14
Fax: (33-4) 78 68 66 45

JERUSALEM • ASHDOD • PARIS • LYON • MONTRÉAL • TORONTO • BUENOS AIRES • MANCHESTER

הרבנות הראשית רמלה

לשכת הרב אבוחצירא רחוב גולומב 25 רמלה טל. 08-9225360

YEHIEL ABUHSSERA
Grand Rabbin de Ramleh
B.P.4 Ramleh
(ISRAEL)

רחוב הראל 48 ת.ד 4 רמלה טל. בית 08-9221122

שאלות חיים

[handwritten Hebrew text]

בברכת התורה ולומדיה
יחיאל אבוחצירא
הרב הראשי לרמלה

[signature]

DAVID R. BANON

Rabbin du Centre Séparade de Laval
Membre du Beth Din de Montréal

רוד רפאל באנון
רוש"ץ יק הספרדי וקאבימדה כלאשאל
חברת דביקמעלאל

[handwritten Hebrew text]

Table of contents

Introduction

The goal of this book is to provide a genuine picture of the true Kabbalah. The study of Kabbalah involves a good comprehension of its general idea, as well as its concepts. The Kabbalah explains often allegorically, the beginning of creation as well as all the dynamic systems that are put in place to interact with man, and for the guidance of the worlds. These systems make us understand the purpose of our actions, their interactions with the superior realms, the hidden messages and meanings in the Torah.

There are different levels of serving and getting closer to the Creator. In the Jewish religion there are many types of prayers and physical acts that we are asked to accomplish regularly, as well as numerous *Mitsvot* – commandments. With a deeper understanding of the reasons and goals of all these actions, one could definitely ascend to a higher level of service and closeness to his Creator. However, this level can not be attained overnight and without a serious investment of time to study and reflecting on this profound knowledge.

In this book, the reader will find most of the basic concepts as well as some more advanced, to get on the right path of truly understanding the Kabbalah. I have also added a glossary of terms and a dictionary of acronyms often found in the Zohar and other Kabbalah texts.

11

I sincerely do hope that this work will help to clarify these concepts and be a good contribution towards an understanding of what is the real Kabbalah.

I would like to thank my wife Simona for her patience and encouragements, Mr. Talib Din for his input on the editing, and my brother Armand for his constant support.

"Blessed are You G-od, teach me your statutes"
(Tehilim, 119, 12).

The Kabbalah

The Kabbalah is the mystical and esoteric explanation of the Torah. It teaches the unfolding of the worlds, the various ways of guidance of these worlds, the role of man in the creation, the will of the Creator and more. No other writings explain in details; the creation of this world and the ones above it, the lights or energies that influence its guidance, nor the final goal of everything. These writings are based on ancient Jewish texts and mostly on the Zohar.

The Kabbalah teaches us that the world is guided by an extremely complex system of forces or lights, which through their interactions provoke chain reactions that impact directly on man and the worlds. Each one of these reactions has numerous ramifications, with many details and results. It explains to us the true guidance of the world, so that we may understand the will of G-od. How and why He created the world, in what way He governs it, the provenance of the souls and angels, the purpose of the existence of evil, the reasons for the dualism of reward and punishment, etc.

The word Kabbalah comes from the verb *Lekabel* (to receive), but to receive it is first necessary to want, and to become a *Keli* (recipient) able to receive and contain this knowledge. The Kabbalah also demonstrates to us the importance of man, because only he, by getting closer to the Creator, can influence these incredible forces. For this, one has to elevate to a higher dimension of understanding, and start asking himself some very important questions like; "Why", "What is the purpose of doing this act or this prayer", "What are the outcomes of my actions" etc.

The other writings explain in the least details "how" to do, but only the Zohar and the Kabbalah explain to us the exact reasons, and effects of all our prayers and actions.

I believe that most yearn to serve at their best the Creator, but have been accustomed to execute and not seek further, or were kept away from this knowledge. It is now the time to know and learn this magnificent science, as it is written and recommended:

> "From there, you shall seek the Lord your G-od, and you shall find him if you seek him with all your heart, and with all your soul."
> (Devarim 4,29)

> "The one, who was able to learn the secrets of the Torah (Kabbalah) and did not make an effort to understand them, will be severely judged"
> (Even Shelomo 85, 24). - HaGra, HaGaon Rabbi Eliyahu de Vilna

> All the souls in this present world, that will make the effort to know their Creator through His secret writings (Kabbalah), will ascend higher than all the other souls that did not learn and understand, and will be first at the time of the resurrection. (Zohar, Vayeshev, 182, 2)

The man who learns Kabbalah is above all the others.
(Zohar, Shemini, 42, 1)

The one that learns Kabbalah to understand the secrets of the Torah, and the purpose of the *Mitsvot* according to the *Sod* (secret), is called a "Son" of the Lord.
(Zohar, Vayera)

And finally, the very clear obligation in the Torah "To know, now", and not just believe:

"וידעת היום והשבת אל-לבבך כי יהו-ה הוא האלה-ים בשמים ממעל ועל-הארץ מתחת אין עוד"

"Know, today, and consider it in your heart, that the Lord is G-od in heaven above and upon the earth beneath, and there is no other."
(Devarim, 4.39)

Chapter 1

CREATION

In the beginning, there was no other existence; the Creator was alone, occupying all space with His light. His light being of such holiness and intensity, it was not possible for any being to exist in its proximity. When He decided to create, He at first had to make a certain distance from His light, to give a possibility of existence to separated beings.

Tsimtsum - retraction

In the beginning, there was no existence except His presence; the Creator was alone, occupying all space with His light[1]. His light, without end, borders or limit, filled everything. He was not bestowing His influence because there was no one to receive it. When He willed to create; He started to influence. His light being of such holiness and intensity, it is not possible for any being to exist in its proximity.

The "*Tsimtsum*" is the first act of *Ein Sof*[2] (Infinite) in the creation. It is the retraction of His light from a certain space and encircling it, so as to reduce its intensity and allow created beings to exist. After this contraction, a ray of His light entered this empty space and formed the first *Sephirot*.

By these boundaries, He revealed the concepts of rigor and limit needed by the created beings, and gave a space for all the created to exist.

See Fig. 1

'Hallal - vacant space

After the *Tsimtsum* (retraction) of His light, an empty space called *'Hallal* was left in the center of this new creation – a space without His full presence. This space is circular and

---

[1] Energie
[2] Without end

19

contains all possibilities of existence for separated entities[3], given that they are now distanced from the intensity of His light.

See Fig. 1

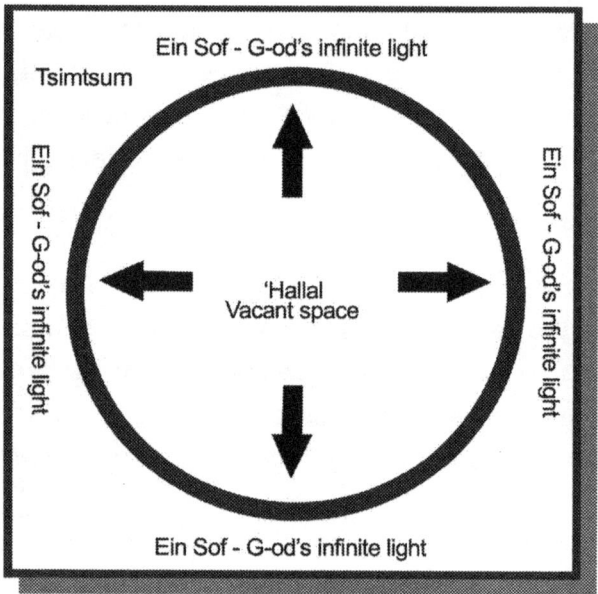

Fig. 1 Tsimtsum – 'Hallal

Reshimu - imprint

When His light retracted to form this round space, a trace of it called *Reshimu* - imprint remained inside. This lower intensity light allowed a space of existence (*Makom*) for all the created worlds and beings.

---

[3] Physical and spiritual

The roots of all future existence and events are in the *Reshimu.* Nothing can come into existence without having its root in this imprint.

The combination of the *Reshimu* - imprint of the original light and the *Kav* – ray of His direct light, will be the origin[4] of all future worlds and existence.

See Fig. 2

Kav - ray

This ray of His direct light called *"Kav"* emerged from *Ein Sof* (Infinite) and entered on one side[5] of the vacant space, where there was still an imprint of the original light. The *Kav,* which represents the masculine and the imprint, the feminine, will now together give existence to the worlds and the various systems of *Sephirot*[6] with which He will govern these worlds.

There are two main systems of guidance of the worlds: one is for the general guidance, in charge of the nature and normal events, and one for men, influenced by their acts and time.

After entering the vacant space, the *Kav* made ten circular *Sephirot* encircling one another - (encircling *Sephirot*) in charge of the general guidance of the worlds. Keeping his

---

[4] Kav is the masculine, Rechimu the feminine
[5] Top
[6] Part of His energy transformed in an attribute or quality. See chapt 2

21

shape, he also made ten *Sephirot* in a linear arrangement - (straight *Sephirot*) in charge of the guidance of the world in the manner of *'Hesed, Din* and *Ra'hamim* (Kindness, rigor and mercy), which is the balanced guidance[7] of this existence.

The *Kav* is the root of all the guidance and the innermost interiority[8] of all this creation.
See Fig. 2

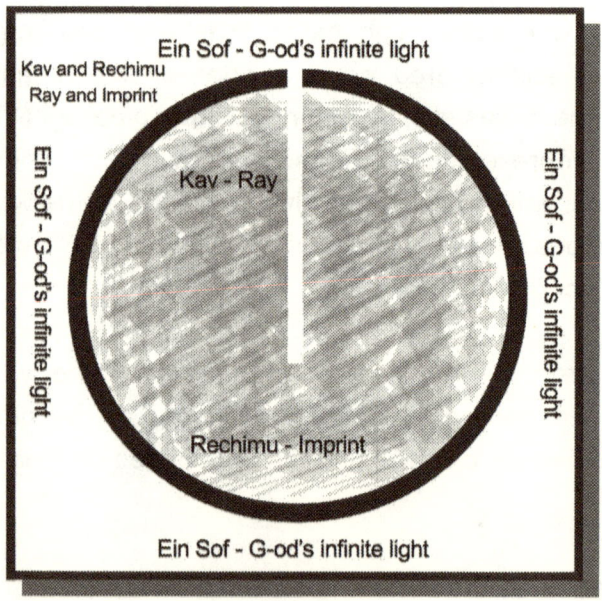

Fig. 2 – *Kav* and *Reshimu*

---

[7] Arranged in three pillars – right, left and center
[8] Being His direct energy

Encircling Sephirot

The ten circular *Sephirot* encircle the whole vacant space, one on the other. The first *Sephira Keter*[9] encircles *'Hokhma*, which encircles *Binah* and so on until *Yesod* encircles the last *Sephira* of *Malkhut*.

These ten circular *Sephirot* are in charge of the general guidance of the worlds, provide for its subsistence, for what is needed for the normal events of nature and for the vegetal and animal life. This guidance is not influenced by the actions of men.

See Fig. 3

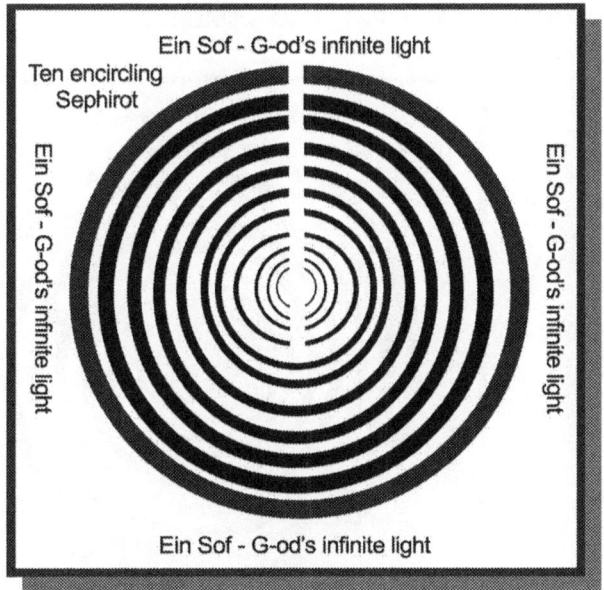

Fig. 3 – Encircling *Sephirot*

---

[9] *Keter* is the outer limit of the vacant space

Straight Sephirot

The *Kav* (ray) maintained his straight shape and made ten other *Sephirot*, but this time in a linear arrangement. They ten straight *Sephirot* were arranged in three columns: right, left and middle, it is the model of the dynamic guidance of the world. Each one of these three columns represents one of the main forces that make the guidance: kindness, rigor and what makes the balance of the two; mercy. This first configuration, or the first world where the emanated lights were formed into ten *Sephirot*, is called *Adam Kadmon* (*Primordial Man*). It is the union between the imprint and the *Kav* (ray). From this first configuration, all the other worlds of *Atsilut* (emanation), *Beriah* (creation), *Yetsirah* (formation) and *'Asiah* (action) came forth into existence.

See fig. 4

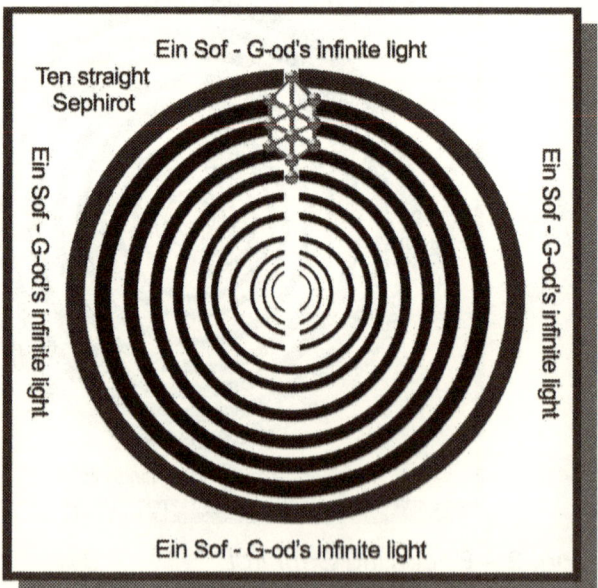

Fig. 4 – Straight Sephirot

Chapter 2

SEPHIROT

The light of G-od is unique and of equal force and quality. A Sephira is in a way a "filter" that transforms this light into a particular force or attribute, by which the Creator guides the worlds.

Sephira

The light of G-od is unique and of equal force and quality. A *Sephira* is in a way a "filter" that holds and transforms a certain part of this light into a particular force or attribute. A *Sephira* is the way the Creator reveals a part, an attribute or a quality of His will in the creation. The light divides into ten different gradations of its original emanation, each with its own qualities, characteristics and actions.

The system of *Sephirot* is one of the main elements studied in the Kabbalah[10]; it describes precisely and with numerous details, the manifestations of the light of G-od and all its emanations by which the Creator guides the worlds.

Each *Sephira* is composed of a vessel[11] called *Keli*, which holds its part of light called *Or*. There is no difference in the *Or* itself, since it is a part of the original light; the difference comes from the particularity, or position of the *Sephira*.

The straight *Sephirot* are arranged in three linear columns: right, left and middle, representing the guidance of the world in the manner of Kindness, rigor and mercy. On the right[12] is the kindness column, on the left, the rigor column and in the middle, the mercy column, which makes the balance[13] between the two other columns. This arrangement of ten

---

[10] Also called Ma'se Hamerkavah – Celestial Chariot
[11] To be understood also as an energy or light, but of a less tenuous consistence
[12] The right always denotes bounty, the left rigor
[13] Mitigates

Sephirot is the concept of all created, as everything that exits is made of ten energies[14].

See Fig. 5

There are ten *Sephirot,* their names are:

Keter	*Crown*	**Tiferet**	*Beauty*
'Hokhma	*Wisdom*	**Netsa'h**	*Glory*
Binah	*Understanding*	**Hod**	*Splendor*
'Hesed	*Bounty*	**Yesod**	*Foundation*
Gevurah	*Rigor*	**Malkhut**	*Kingship*

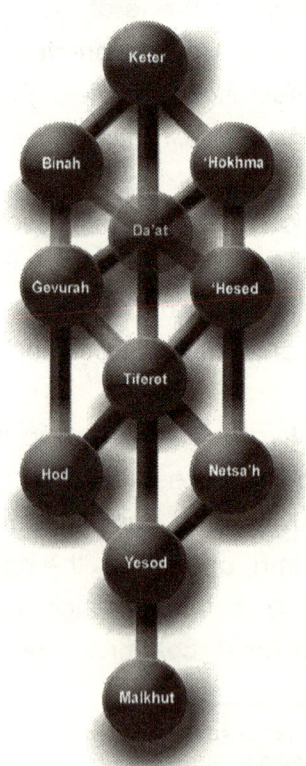

Fig. 5

---

[14] Also arranged in three pillars

On the right: the kindness (*'Hesed*) column with the *Sephirot 'Hokhma, 'Hesed, and Netsa'h.*

In the middle: the mercy (*Ra'hamim*) *column* with the *Sephirot Keter, Tiferet, Yesod, and Malkhut*

On the left: the rigor (*Din*) column with the *Sephirot Binah, Gevurah, and Hod.*

There is one more *Sephira* called *Da'at*, also in the mercy column, which is counted when *Keter* is not[15].

Keter - Crown

The first and most important of the *Sephirot* is *Keter*. It is complete kindness to all, even to the non - deserving. Like a crown that is above the head, it is not a part of the body, but represents the glory that is granted to whom it is on. The *Sephira Keter* encompasses all the other *Sephirot* and represents the divine will, its first expression and manifestation.

---

[15] They are never more than ten

Its position is at the top of the center column, which corresponds to mercy. From it, are made the two most important *Partsufim* - configurations: *'Atik Yomin* and *Arikh Anpin*.

Its corresponding name is *AHY- H-* אהי-ה

Its corresponding *Miluy* (spelling)[16] of name: *'A"V* - עב (72). The level of the soul associated with *Keter* is *Ye'hida,* its highest level. Its physical correspondence is the head

'Hokhma - Wisdom

The second *Sephira, 'Hokhma,* is also kindness to all, even to the non - deserving, but less than *Keter,* and not always. *Keter* being the will, *'Hokhma* is the first manifestation of the thought. It is the initial consciousness in its general form.

Its position is on top of the right column, which corresponds to *'Hesed* (Kindness). From it, is made the configuration *Abah*.

_____

[16] One of the four different spellings of the four letters of the name י-ה-ו-ה

Its corresponding name is *YH - ה-י*, and its corresponding *Miluy* (spelling) of name is *'A"V -עב (72)*.

Its physical correspondence is the right brain and its corresponding level of the soul is *'Haya*.

Binah

The third *Sephira, Binah,* is kindness to all, even to the less deserving, but from her, the rigors start[17]. After the initial consciousness in *'Hokhma*, the role of *Binah* is to translate this general thought into a cognitive mode ready to be put in action.

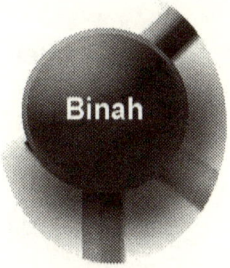

Its position is at the top of the left column, which corresponds to *Din* (rigor). From it is made the configuration *Imah*.

Its corresponding name is *YHV-H   ה-ו-ה-י* (but with the vowels of *Elokim),* and its corresponding *Miluy* (spelling) of name is *SaG (63) - גo*. Its physical correspondence is the left brain and its corresponding level of the soul is *Neshama*.

---

[17] Being on the left pillar

Da'at

It is the fourth of the *Sephirot*, *Da'at* is counted when *Keter* is not. Its quality is the guidance that makes the equilibrium between *'Hokhma and Binah.*

Its position is at the center of the center column, which corresponds to *'Ra'hamim (*mercy).
Its corresponding name is *AHV-H* – אהו-ה

Its role is mainly to make the *Mo'hin*[18] - directive force for configurations *Z'A*[19] and *Nukva.*

'Hesed

The fourth *Sephira*, *'Hesed,* is complete kindness but to whom it is deserving. It is the quality of always giving and without limits, caring, expanding and reaching outwards to help and forgive. An excess of kindness becomes negative,

---

[18] See chapt. 5 - *Partsufim*
[19] *Zeir Anpin*

as it could permit everything and anything without restriction, not wanting to punish.

Its position is in the middle of the right column, which corresponds to *'Hesed* (kindness). It is one of the *Sephirot* that make the configuration *Z'A*.
Its corresponding name is *El–* אל

Its corresponding *Miluy* (spelling) of name is *MaH* (מה) 45. Its physical correspondence is the right arm and its corresponding level of the soul is *Rua'h*.

Gevurah

The fifth *Sephira, Gevurah*[20]*,* is full rigor to whom it is deserving. It is the quality of restriction, limitation and severity. It restricts the excess of kindness of *Sephira 'Hesed*, but is still influenced by it, fortunately, because complete rigor will be the destruction of anything not perfect.

---

[20] Rigor

Its position is in the middle of the left column, which corresponds to *Din* (rigor). It is one of the *Sephirot* that make the configuration *Z'A*.

Its corresponding name is *Elohi-m*[21] אלהי-ם

Its corresponding *Miluy* (spelling) of name is *MaH* (מה) 45. Its physical correspondence is the left arm, and its corresponding level of the soul is *Rua'h*.

Tiferet

The sixth *Sephira, Tiferet,* is kindness and justice that make the equilibrium between the *Sephirot 'Hesed* and *Gevurah*, between complete kindness and rigor. It is represented as the thorax in a body, which holds and maintains all the other members in their respective place.

---

[21] This name of G-od also denotes rigor

Its position is in the middle of the center column, which corresponds to *Ra'hamim* (mercy). It is one of the *Sephirot* that make the configuration *Z'A*.
Its corresponding name is *YHV-K* י-ה-ו-ה

Its corresponding *Miluy* (spelling) of name is *MaH* (מה) 45. Its physical correspondence is the thorax, and its corresponding level of the soul is *Rua'h*.

Netsa'h

The seventh *Sephira, Netsa'h,* is diminished kindness to whom it is deserving. It receives from *Sephira Tiferet* the new mitigated reality between *Sephirot 'Hesed* and *Gevurah*, but drawn on the side of kindness, since *Netsa'h* is on the right column of bounty.

Its position is at the bottom of the right column, which corresponds to *'Hesed* (kindness). It is one of the *Sephirot* that make the configuration *Z'A*. Its corresponding name is YKVK *Tsebaot* יהו-ה -צבאות

35

Its corresponding *Miluy* (spelling) of name is *MaH* (45) (מה).
Its physical correspondence is the right leg, and its
corresponding level of the soul is *Rua'h.*

Hod

The eighth *Sephira, Hod,* is diminished rigor to whom it is
deserving. It also receives from *Sephira Tiferet* the new
mitigated reality between *Sephirot 'Hesed* and *Gevurah*, but
drawn on the rigor side, since *Hod* is on the left column of
rigor.

Its position is at the bottom of the left column, which
corresponds to *Din* (rigor). It is one of the *Sephirot* that make
the configuration *Z'A.*

Its corresponding name is *Elohi-m Tsebaot*
אלהי-ם -צבאות

Its corresponding *Miluy* (spelling) of name is *MaH* (45) (מה).
Its physical correspondence is the left leg, and its
corresponding level of the soul is *Rua'h.*

Yesod

The ninth *Sephira, Yesod*, makes the equilibrium between *Sephira Netsa'h* and *Hod* for the guidance and is the link or connection between all the superior *Sephirot* and the *Sephira Malkhut*. It is the point of convergence between the superior realms and the last *Sephira* of *Malkhut*, which will reflect the outflows of energies to man and the creation.

Its position is before the last *Sephira*, at the bottom of the center column, which corresponds to *Ra'hamim* (mercy). It is one of the *Sephirot* that make the configuration *Z'A*.
Its corresponding name is *Shada- y --* שד-י

Its corresponding *Miluy* (spelling) of name is *MaH* (45) (מה).
Its physical correspondence is the masculine organ, and its corresponding level of the soul is *Rua'h.*

Malkhut

The tenth *Sephira, Malkhut,* translates all the superior emanations that are channeled through *Sephira Yesod* into one that is reflected to the creation. It is the link or connection between all the superior *Sephirot* and man. This relationship is bidirectional, as all that is communicated from below to the higher *Sephirot* will first go to *Malkhut,* and from it, to the *Sephirot* above it.

Its position is at the bottom of the center column, which corresponds to *Ra'hamim* (mercy). It makes the configuration *Nukva,* divided in two *Partsufim: Ra'hel* and *Leah.*
Its corresponding name is *Adona-y —'-אדנ*

Its corresponding *Miluy* of name is *BaN (52) - בנ.* Its physical correspondence is the crown on the masculine organ and its corresponding level of the soul is *Nefesh.*

Each one of the ten *Sephirot* consists of another ten *Sephirot*, which also comprise of ten, and again of ten etc. *See fig. 6*

As for example there is:
'Hesed of *Gevurah*, or
Hod of *'Hesed* of *Gevurah*, or
Yesod of *Hod* of *'Hesed* of *Gevurah* etc

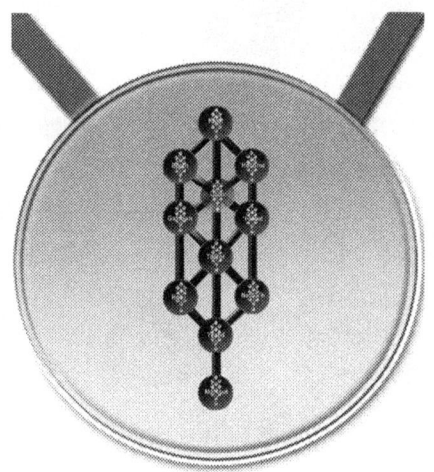

Fig. 6

For certain types of actions the *Sephirot* divide in groups of which makes three triplets:

'HBD[22] - *'Hokhma, Binah* and *Da'at*
'HGT[23] – *'Hesed, Gevurah* and *Tiferet*
NHY[24] – *Netsa'h Hod* and *Yesod*

---

[22] Pronounced as *'HaBad*
[23] *'HaGat*
[24] *NeHY*

The first triplet of the *Sephirot, 'HBD - 'Hokhma, Binah and Da'at,* acts together as the highest level of the guiding force - *Mo'hin* for a lower configuration, and are called the *Mo'hin* of growth. They usually come after the *'HGT* and *NHY.*

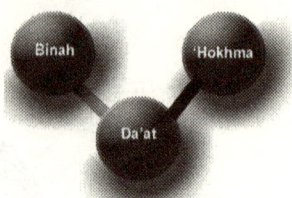

The second triplet of the *Sephirot, HGT - 'Hesed, Gevurah and Tiferet,* acts together as the second level of the guiding force - *Mo'hin* for a lower configuration. They usually come after *NHY* and before *'HBD.*

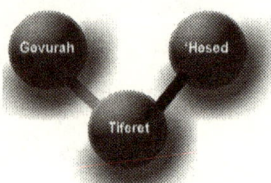

The third triplet of the *Sephirot, NHY - Netsa'h, Hod and Yesod* mostly act together as the third or interior guiding force - *Mo'hin* for the lower configuration. They come and enter before all the others, i.e. before *'HGT* and *'HBD.*

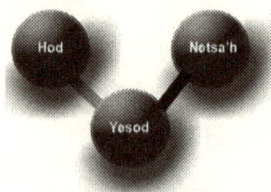

There are also configurations of one or more *Sephirot* acting in coordination, which are called *Partsufim.*

Chapter 3

ADAM KADMON

The first configuration, or the first world where the emanated lights were formed into ten Sephirot, is called Adam Kadmon (Primordial Man).

Primordial man

This first configuration[25] is the first world where the emanated lights were formed into ten straight *Sephirot*. The linear arrangement of three columns - right, left and middle - represents the guidance of the world in the manner of Kindness, rigor and mercy. This first emanation is the origin of all future emanations.

Adam Kadmon being at such close proximity to the *Ein Sof*, we cannot grasp anything of its nature. Our understanding only starts from the emanations that came out of him[26] by the way of his senses, which are called his branches.

These four branches are metaphorically called sight, hearing, smell and speech. They spread out from his eyes, ears, nose, and mouth. In the language of Kabbalah, we use names of body parts solely to illustrate the esoteric powers

---

[25] Made of the Kav and Rechimu – Ray and imprint
[26] To make all the lower worlds

of these forces. It is understood, of course, that there is no physical existence at these levels. When we say ears, mouth, or any other physical expression, the goal is to describe the inner sense, or the position they represent.

To identify[27] these creative lights or emanations that came out of *Adam Kadmon*, the Kabbalah describes them with the main name of G-od י-ה-ו-ה, and the various letters added to make its different spellings.

Spelling - Miluyim

These creative forces or energies are the different powers invested in the four letters of the name of G-od י-ה-ו-ה, and the various spellings of each letter. Since each Hebrew letter also has a different numerical value with the different ways of spelling it, the total of the name changes, (72, 63, 45 or 52) and each one of these names has now a different identity and action, depending on which letters are used. Each one of these possibilities is different in nature and action[28].

The letters that are added for the different spellings of the letters are[29] י ה ו א ד

---

[27] All creations are from emanations of the energy of the name י-ה-ו-ה
[28] And individual emanations
[29] These letters add to the four letters י-ה-ו- ה to make the spellings

The different spellings of the letters are as follows:

- The letter י *(Yud)* can only be spelled one way יוד
- The letter ה *(He)* can be spelled with a י *(Yud)*, an א *(Aleph)*, or a ה *(He)* הי–הא-הה *(He)*
- The letter ו *(Vav)* can be spelled with a וי *(Yud and Vav)*, or with או *(Aleph and Vav)*, or with a ו *(Vav)* ואו-וו-ויו

The four *Miluyim* (spellings) are:
- בן , מה , סג, עב - *'A"V, SaG, MaH, BaN*

		ה	ו	ה	י		
'A"V	עב	הי	ויו	הי	יוד		
		15	22	15	20	=	72
SaG	סג	הי	ואו	הי	יוד		
		15	13	15	20	=	63
MaH	מה	הא	ואו	הא	יוד		
		6	13	6	20	=	45
BaN	בן	הה	וו	הה	יוד		
		10	12	10	20	=	52

Each name can also be divided and subdivided as:
'A"V of 'A"V, SaG of 'A"V, MaH of 'A"V ...
BaN of BaN of SaG, SaG of MaH of 'A"V etc.

עב	סג	מה	בן
'A'V	SaG	MaH	BaN
'A'V	'A'V	'A'V	'A'V
SaG	SaG	SaG	SaG
MaH	MaH	MaH	MaH
BaN	BaN	BaN	BaN

The name *'A"V* is of the highest level of the four names. Its *Miluy* is with the letter ' (*Yud*) for a total of 72.

	ה	ו	ה	י	
עב *'A'V*	הי	ויו	הי	יוד	
	15	22	15	20	= 72

The name *SaG* is the second level of the four names. Its *Miluy* is with the letter ' (*Yud*) and א (*Aleph*) for a total of 63.

	ה	ו	ה	י	
סג *SaG*	הי	ואו	הי	יוד	
	15	13	15	20	= 63

The name *MaH (45)* is the third level of the four names. Its *Miluy* is with the letter א (*Aleph*) for a total of 45.

	ה	ו	ה	י	
מה *MaH*	הא	ואו	הא	יוד	
	6	13	6	20	= 45

The name *BaN (52)* is the fourth level of the four names. Its *Miluy* is with the letter ו (*Vav*) for a total of 52.

	ה	ו	ה	י
BaN בן	הה	וו	הה	יוד
	10	12	10	20 = 52

All the emanations and *Sephirot* that emerged from *Adam Kadmon* by way of his apertures[30] of his face, were of the various aspects of these four names.

They have different actions and *Tikunim,* and all the *Partsufim (configurations)* will be constructed by their union.

From the ears, nose and mouth emerge *Sephirot* - lights of the aspect of the name *SaG* (63).

From the eyes, emerged *Sephirot* - lights of the aspect of the name *BaN (52).* These feminine lights caused the *Shvirat HaKelim* (breaking of the vessels).

From the forehead, *Sephirot* - lights of the aspect of the name of *MaH* (45) emerged; these masculine lights will make the *Tikun* (rectification) of the broken *Sephirot*, and together with *BaN (52)* make all the *Partsufim* (configurations) for the guidance of the worlds.

---

[30] These emanations came out from inside Adam Kadmon

These emanations caused certain states of existence or worlds. The emanations that came out from the mouth made a world called *'Olam Ha'akudim* – the world of the attached. The ones that came out from the eyes made *'Olam HaniKudim* - the world of points. The emanations from the forehead made the *'Olam HaBerudim* – world of the *Tikun* (reparation).

From these emanations, the other four worlds of *Atsilut* (emanation), *Beriah* (creation), *Yetsirah* (formation) and *'Asiah* (action) will unfold.

World of the attached – 'Olam Ha'akudim

In the world of the attached, when the *Sephirot* emerged for the first time from the mouth of *Adam Kadmon*, they did not have an individual recipient, but one unique recipient for all.

The seven lower *Sephirot* were aligned one under the other in a straight line and not in the three pillar arrangement. Therefore, they were not ready for the guidance of kindness, rigor and mercy. *See fig. 7*

Fig. 7

This type of configuration could not remain, the most tenuous part of the lights returned to their origin in the mouth, but not completely, each one leaving its trace. The parts of the lights that remained thickened, but were still illuminated by their own parts that ascended. The ones that remained and the trace of the ones that ascended, struck each other and produced sparks that formed the recipients for the more tenuous lights that will return a second time, so the *Sephirot* will be complete; light and recipient for each.

This is considered as an annulment, but not as important as the one of the world of points.

World of points – 'Olam Hanikudim

After the emanations from the mouth of *Adam Kadmon*, ten *Sephirot* came out through his eyes[31]; they were of the aspects of the feminine name of *BaN (52)*. This world is called the world of points because these *Sephirot* had their own recipients, but were separated, with no attachment or relation to each other. Therefore, unable to hold the influx of their lights, the seven lower recipients broke and were separated from their lights. *See fig 8*

They correspond to the feminine aspect - rigor, and are the root of deterioration. When they came out, the first three *Sephirot - KHB (Keter, 'Hokhma, Binah)*, took strength from

---

[31] No more open aperture on the face was available

49

the lights of the ears, nose and mouth of *Adam Kadmon*[32] and were able to stand in three columns. However, the seven lower *Sephirot,* who took only from the lights of the mouth, could not stand in this order and broke. This is called *Shvirat HaKelim* (breaking of the vessels)[33]; this imperfect arrangement is the first origin of the *Sitra A'hra* or "evil"[34].

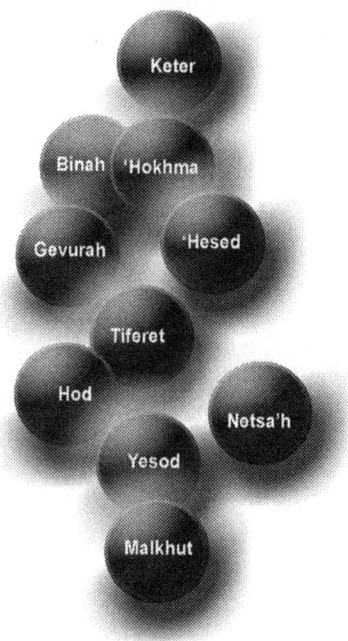

Fig. 8

---

[32] When coming down, these lights went through the higher preceding lights
[33] See chapt. 4 – Breaking of the vessels
[34] Opposite negative force

World of reparation – 'Olam HaBerudim

This is also called *'Olam HaTikun*[35]. The *Tikun* (rectification) was done by the union of the *Sephirot* of *BaN (52)* (rigor) with the *Sephirot* of *MaH (45)* (mercy) that came out of the forehead of *Adam Kadmon.* By this union, the feminine *BaN (52)* was repaired by the masculine *MaH (45)* and together made the *Partsufim* (configurations). With this new arrangement[36], the *Sephirot* were able to stand in the three-column configuration of kindness, rigor and mercy.

This *Tikun* of the arrangement of the *Sephirot* into three columns will allow the beginning of the construction of the first *Partsufim*.

---

[35] Not completely repaired, but enough for a possibily of existence.
[36] All the *Sephirot* are made of these two aspects

51

Chapter 4

BREAKING OF THE VESSELS

The seven lower Sephirot of the name of BaN were not in the three pillar arrangement needed for the direction of Kindness, rigor and mercy. Therefore, they could not hold the influx of their lights and broke. If they had contained their lights, the world would have been in a perfect state from the start.

53

Breaking of the vessels
Shvirat HaKelim

At the creation, all the creative forces[37] were invested in the configuration *Adam Kadmon.* They emerged in different emanations from the apertures in his face for the construction of the worlds.

The ten Sephirot that came out from his eyes were of the aspect of the name of *BaN (52);* they correspond to the feminine aspect - rigor, and are the root of deterioration. When they came out, the recipients of the first three *Sephirot* of *Keter,* '*Hokhma* and *Binah* received and contained their lights, because they were in the three-column arrangement

The seven lower recipients of the *Sephirot* were not in the three pillar arrangement needed for the direction of Kindness, rigor and mercy. The lights tried to enter in their respective recipients, but their force was overwhelming and, unable to hold their lights the recipients broke. The lights stayed in the world of *Atsilut,* their recipients fell to the lower worlds.

This caused an important damage called *Shvirat HaKelim* – *the breaking of the vessels.* The recipients of the seven *Sephirot,* which did not contain their lights, fell to the world of *Beriah* (creation). This imperfect arrangement is the first

---

[37] Energies in the four letters ot the name ה-ו-ה-י and their composed names

55

origin of damage and of the *Sitra A'hra* (negative side) - "evil".

The three first *Sephirot Keter, 'Hokhma,* and *Binah* did not completely contain their lights in their lower parts; they fell lower[38] but did not break. These lower parts correspond to what is needed for the guidance of the seven lower *Sephirot,* if they had completely contained their lights, the seven *Sephirot* would not have broken, and the notions of *Kilkul* (damage) and *Tikun* (repair) would not exist[39]. The roots of all the created are in the seven lower *Sephirot (Za'T)*; the three first *Sephirot* are like a crown on the other seven to repair and direct them.

It is important to understand that all that happens in our world is similar to what occurred in this fall. If the recipients had contained their lights, the seven lower *Sephirot* would not have broken and the world would have been in a perfect state from the start.

The separation between *G'aR* (three first *Sephirot*), which are considered the head -directive forces, and *Za'T* (the seven lower *Sephirot*), - the body, is comparable to the death of man, when his soul departs and ascends, while his body descends into the earth and he is no more alive. The light that gives life to the recipient is comparable to the soul that keeps the body alive.

---

[38] In *Atsilut*
[39] The worlds would have been in a perfect state at the start

Sparks

To sustain the recipients after they broke, 288[40] sparks[41] of the lights came down as well, because a connection to their original lights was needed to keep them alive. Some of these sparks reunited with their higher lights, and helped the recipients rise and also reunite with their lights, while others fell even lower into the other worlds.

The *Tikun* – reparation is to make rise all the other sparks to their origin and bring back the creation to its original state. Therefore, the goal of all the works, deeds and prayers of men in this existence is to help and participate in the ascent of the rest of the fallen 288 sparks to their origin. This can be done different ways but mainly by accomplishing the *Mitsvot* and by the prayers.

After the breaking of the *Kelim* and the separation from their lights, it was necessary for the guidance of the world that reparation be done. From the forehead of *Adam Kadmon* emerged ten *Sephirot* of the aspect of the name of *MaH (45),* corresponding to the masculine - reparation. This is in contrast to the *Sephirot* of *BaN (52), which* correspond to the feminine aspect - rigor, and are the root of deterioration.

The *Tikun* was done by the union of the *Sephirot* of *MaH (45)* (mercy) and *BaN (52)* (rigor) in complex arrangements, so as to allow the feminine *BaN (52)* to be repaired by the masculine *MaH (45),* and for the *Sephirot* to stand in the

---

[40] 288 main sparks which subdivide number ot times
[41] Parts of energies

three-column arrangement of kindness, rigor and mercy. With the proper order of the *Sephirot* in place, various configurations that are called *Partsufim* completed the creation.

With the emanation of the lights of *MaH (45)* He could have done the *Tikun* (rectification) of all the worlds after the *Shvirat HaKelim (breaking of the vessels)*, but then, there would not have been a reason for the participation of man in this *Tikun*.

It is to give a possibility to man to act and repair the creation that G-od restrained in a way, his outflow of kindness to this world. At the completion of this *Tikun* of unification between the fallen sparks and their *Kelim*[42], it will be the time of the resurrection of the dead and the arrival of *Moshia'h*.

---

[42] Recipients of the *Sephirot*

Chapter 5

PARTSUFIM

A Partsuf is a configuration of one or more Sephirot acting in coordination. The guidance of the world is dependent on the different positioning and interactions of the masculine and feminine Partsufim - configurations, since they have a direct effect on the *measure and balance of the factors of kindness, rigor and mercy.*

Partsufim - configuration

The light of G-od is of a perfect unicity, without any variables or difference. Once this energy enters a particular *Sephira*[43], its outcome or effect is transformed into a particular force or attribute by which the Creator guides the worlds. A *Partsuf* is a configuration[44] of one or more *Sephirot* acting in coordination. *Partsuf* in Aramaic means face, visage or countenance. A face is composed of many and various elements as eyes, nose, mouth, forehead and so on, but all are coordinated as one single unit. A face is also unique[45]; it shows the particular identity of a person and is the main vehicle of communication.

Some *Partsufim* - configurations are masculine and bestow kindness, while others are feminine and bestow rigor. The masculine corresponds to kindness - *'Hesed* and is of the aspect of the name of *MaH (45)*. The feminine corresponds to rigor - *Gevurah* and is of the aspect of the name of *BaN (52)*. By their unions[46], different equilibriums of these two forces (Kindness and rigor), make the guidance. Complete rigor would be the destruction of anything not perfect, while complete kindness would permit everything without restrictions. However, these two aspects are necessary for the guidance of justice, and to give man the possibility of free choice.

---

[43] The transformation is caused by the *Sephira*, the energy is unique and does not change
[44] Arrangement of one or more *Sephirot* in ten *Sephirot*
[45] Each *Partsuf* – configuration has its own unique identity and role
[46] See *Zivug* –union

The *Partsufim* - configurations are in a constant state of action, illuminations and inter-relations between them. This dynamism of exchange and influence of energies is called *Tikunim*[47] of the *Partsufim*. These *Tikunim* result in various illuminations of different intensities, depending on time and the actions of man. They translate the upper will into particular influences and effects, for the guidance of the worlds.

The construction of a *Partsuf* - configuration is achieved by way of a *Zivug* (union) of two higher masculine and feminine *Partsufim*, followed by a period called gestation inside the higher feminine configuration, and birth, when it is revealed. There is afterwards the suckling, where it is nursing energies from the higher *Partsufim*, and finally the growth when it is now fully independent.[48]

There are five main[49] *Partsufim* - configurations:

- *Arikh Anpin* - :Long countenance
- *Abah* - Father
- *Imah* - Mother
- *Zeir Anpin* - Small countenance
- *Nukva* - Feminine

And one above them: *'Atik Yomin* (clothed inside *Arikh Anpin*).

---

[47] Actions or outcomes
[48] Man was created at the image of the supernal energies
[49] Also secondary configurations

From these five main configurations emerge seven more. They all emanate from the ten *Sephirot* as follows:

From *Keter*:
- *'Atik Yomin* and his ***Nukva***
- ***Arikh Anpin*** and his ***Nukva***

From *'Hokhma*:
 - ***Abah***
- From *Malkhut* of *Abah* - ***Israel Saba***
- From *Malkhut* of *Israel Saba* - ***Israel Saba* 2**

From *Binah*:
- ***Imah***
- From *Malkhut* of *Imah*-***Tevunah***
- From *Malkhut* of *Tevunah* - ***Tevunah* 2**

Israel Saba and *Tevunah* are also called by their initials *ISOT* or *ISOT* 2.

From *'Hesed, Gevurah, Tiferet, Netsa'h, Hod, and Yesod*:
 - ***Zeir Anpin*** also called ***Israel***
From *Zeir Anpin* - ***Ya'acov***

From *Malkhut*:
Nukva, divided in two *Partsufim*: ***Ra'hel* and Leah**

63

Configuration 'Atik Yomin

The configuration *'Atik Yomin* is superior to all the configurations. It has ten *Sephirot*. His aspect of the name of *MaH (45)* corresponds to the masculine principle; his aspect of the name of *BaN (52)* corresponds to the feminine. He is called *'Atik* and his *Nukva*. His *Nukva* – feminine is attached to him, her back to his back. *'Atik* is thus all face, facing to the back, his feminine configuration, facing to the front, his masculine configuration. Each one of these aspects – masculine and feminine – is comprised of ten *Sephirot*.

'Atik's masculine aspect is not clothed inside the first world of *Atsilut*. The first three of the ten *Sephirot* of his *Nukva* - feminine aspect - are above *Atsilut* and together make the *Radl'a* - רישה דלא אתידע (the unknown head). [50]

His seven lower feminine *Sephirot* attach to the world below and dress inside configuration *Arikh Anpin* in the following manner: *'Hesed* of *'Atik* in *Keter* of *Arikh, Gevurah* in *'Hokhma, Tiferet* in *Binah*. His three *Sephirot* of *NHY* (*Netsa'h, Hod, Yesod*) have three parts each: the first part of *NHY* in *'Hesed, Gevurah* and *Tiferet,* the second part of *NHY* in *Netsa'h, Hod* and *Yesod,* the third part of *NH* (*Netsa'h, Hod*), and *Malkhut* of *'Atik* in *Malkhut* of *Arikh Anpin.*

---

[50] The outcomes of its actions are above our understanding

The lower *Sephira* of a world makes the connection with the world below it and becomes its configuration *'Atik*[51]. In *Atsilut,* it is the *Malkhut* of *Adam Kadmon* that becomes its configuration *'Atik.* It is the same in the three other worlds of *Beriah, Yetsirah* and *'Asiah,* the *Malkhut* of the world above becomes the configuration *'Atik* of the world below.

Configuration Arikh Anpin

Arikh Anpin is the main configuration in each world; all the other configurations are his "branches". He and his feminine make one configuration; called *Arikh Anpin* and his *Nukva.* His masculine is his right side, his feminine, his left. *Arikh Anpin* is the first configuration in *Atsilut* and the root of all the others.

Arikh Anpin is different from the other configurations, his first three *Sephirot,* which are called his three heads, are not in the three column arrangement; his *Sephira Binah* is under *Keter* and *'Hokhma,* which are in a straight line. *See fig. 9*

Arikh Anpin reaches from the top to the bottom of a world. *Abah* and *Imah* dress his right and left arm (his *Sephira 'Hesed* and *Gevurah*); their *Keter* reach his *Sephira Binah* and their *Malkhut* his *Sephira Tiferet.*
See fig. 10

---

[51] There is continuity of attachment and communication in all the worlds

65

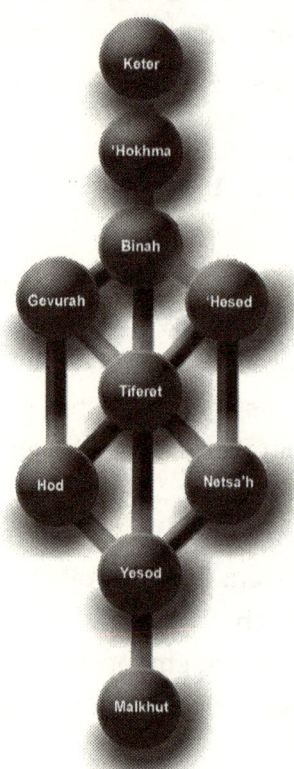

Fig. 9

Arikh Anpin has three heads, which are the roots of the direction of kindness, rigor and mercy. The first is *Keter*, the second is in the space between his *Keter* and *'Hokhma,* the third one is his *'Hokhma.* Their names are:

1- *Gulgolta* - his *Keter*
2- *Avirah* - in the space between his *Keter* and *'Hokhma*
3- *Mo'ha* - his *'Hokhma*

These three heads emanate from *Arikh Anpin* to the configurations *Abah* and *Imah,* and from there, to configuration *Z'A*[52]. The emanations and actions of configuration *Arikh Anpin* are called his *Tikunim*

Other *Tikunim* – emanations of energies and actions – come out from the face of *Sephira 'Hokhma* of *Arikh Anpin* and spread downward; they are called allegorically his hair, or beard. They divide into thirteen and are called the thirteen *Tikunim* of the *Dikna* - the beard of *Arikh Anpin*. These emanations are called hair and beard because they spread out in individual conduits.

The other *Tikunim,* emanations of lights from *Arikh Anpin,* are for the attainment and abundance. However, the guidance itself is from the *Dikna,* lights of the beard, and it is through it that the abundance flows.

Configurations Abah and Imah

These two *Partsufim* (configurations) are essential for the guidance of the worlds; they are the link between configuration *Arikh Anpin,* which is the highest configuration, and configuration *Zeir Anpin* who communicates these emanations to the worlds by his *Zivug* (union) with the configuration *Nukva*. *Abah* is the *Sephira 'Hokhma,* and *Imah* the *Sephira Binah.*

---

[52] From Z'A to *Nukva* and then to the world

They emanated by the *Zivug (union)* of configuration *Arikh Anpin* with his *Nukva* (feminine). *Abah* is the masculine aspect and *Imah* the feminine. They are influenced and built by the lights of configuration *Arikh* and are at the level of his arms – *Sephirot 'Hesed* and *Gevurah*. *Abah* is on the right - *Sephira 'Hesed*, and *Imah* on the left - *Sephira Gevurah*. See fig. 10

To communicate their emanations, *Abah* and *Imah* unite to emanate their influence. There are for *Abah* and *Imah* two types of *Zivug* (unions): the constant *Zivug* is called exterior and is for the subsistence of the worlds[53], while the second is called interior and is for the renewing of the *Mo'hin* - guiding force of *Z"uN (Zeir Anpin and Nukva)*.

The *Sephira Malkhut* of *Abah* becomes another configuration called *Israel Saba*. Similarly, *Malkhut* of *Imah* becomes another configuration called *Tevunah*. These two secondary configurations act as an extension of *Abah* and *Imah* to transmit a reduced intensity of their emanations. They are mostly called by their initials *ISoT*. They themselves have their own secondary configurations called *Israel Saba 2* and *Tevunah 2* – *ISoT 2*. They transmit an even more reduced intensity of the emanations of *Abah* and *Imah*. See fig. 10

---

[53] Not influenced by the actions of men

The main role of *Abah* and *Imah* is to give to configuration *Z'A*, his *Mo'hin* – guiding force[54]. There are different states of growth for configuration *Z'A*. In its first growth, he receives his *Mo'hin* - guiding force from the configurations *ISOT* (*Israel Saba* and *Tevunah*), and in his second more important growth, he receives them directly from *Abah* and *Imah*.

Configuration Zeir Anpin

Configuration *Zeir Anpin* is most often called by his initials; *Z'A*. He is composed of the six lower *Sephirot: 'Hesed, Gevurah, Tiferet, Netsa'h, Hod,* and *Yesod.*[55] For the created, Z'A with configuration *Nukva* are the main configurations for the guidance. All our relationships with the above are first directed to *Z'uN* (*Zeir Anpin* and *Nukva*).

Zeir Anpin is a dynamic configuration, constantly in a process of getting from a weaker state to one of growth to renew its forces and influence. At first, *Z'A* is incomplete having only seven *Sephirot,* and in a state of *Tardema* (somnolence). Inside of *Imah*, *Z'A* goes through a period of gestation, followed by a first period of infancy and a first growth. To act, he needs to get his *Mo'hin* – directive force, which are his three first *Sephirot* of *"Hokhma, Binah* and *Da'at,* and get to a stage of growth. They are given to him in a specific order from the configurations above him; *ISOT* or *Abah* and *Imah*.

---

[54] Their three *Sephirot- Netsa'h, Hod* and *Yesod*
[55] Becomes ten *Sephirot* when he gets his guiding force

During the time of the gestation, *Z'A* is not really acting for it is being built. At the time of suckling it starts to act, and at the growth stage it is ready to act and influence.

When the three *Sephirot* of *NHY (Netsa'h, Hod, Yesod)* of *ISOT* 2 are the directive force of *Z'A*, it is at the stage of the first growth. But when *NHY* of *ISOT* 1 are clothed in him, it is considered as if *Abah* and *Imah* were clothed in him directly as his *Mo'hin* – directive force, and this stage is the second growth. It is only after the second growth that *Z'A* reaches its full potential. This is called *Gadlut* 2.

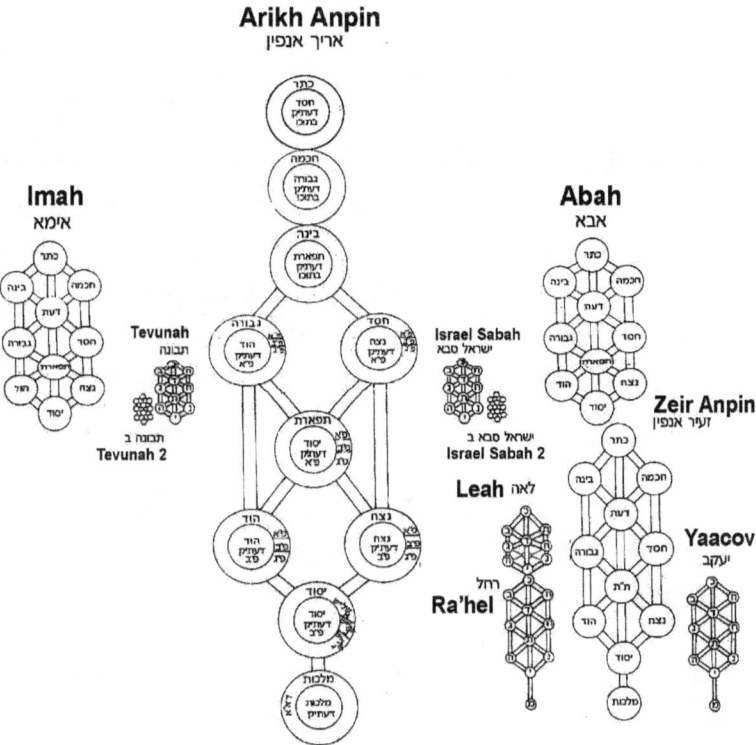

Fig, 10

Mo'hin – directive force

The Mo'hin[56] are the directive force given to a configuration by one or two superior configurations. Depending on the state of growth[57], there are Mo'hin of Katnut – infancy - and of Gadlut – growth. There are also Mo'hin that enter the lower configuration – interior, and Mo'hin that encircle him - exterior. These directive forces vary in strength and intensities.

During gestation, the directive force are at the lowest level and are called NHY (Netsa'h, Hod, Yesod) of the Mo'hin; they are of the aspect of Nefesh.

During the suckling, the lights grow and the directive force are at a higher level; they are called HGT ('Hesed, Gevurah, Tiferet) of the Mo'hin and are of the aspect of Rua'h.

During growth, the directive forces are now fully developed to guide with the full force of HBD ('Hokhma, Binah, Da'at); they are of the aspect of Neshama.

Two distinct Mo'hin come to Z'A: directive forces of Imah arrive first, and then the directive forces of Abah, second. The directive forces that are given from Abah and from Imah to Z'A, are called his Tselem (צלם) and do not completely enter into him

---

[56] Brains - intelligence
[57] First or second

The ones that enter inside the lower configuration – interior, are the three *Sephirot NHY (Netsa'h, Hod, Yesod)* of the superior configuration, they divide in three and are now composed of nine parts and correspond to the צ. They spread into the nine *Sephirot* of *Z'A*.

The ones that do not enter are *HBD, HGT* of the higher configuration. They do not enter inside the lower configuration, but rather encircle him on the outside in the three-column arrangement of kindness, rigor and mercy. The encircling *Mo'hin* are of a higher aspect than the interior *Mo'hin* and correspond to the לם of the complete *Mo'hin* - צלם

The *HGT ('Hesed, Gevurah, Tiferet)* that surround him correspond to the ל
The *KHBD (Keter, 'Hokhma, Binah, Da'at)* that encircle him correspond to the ם

Before reaching its full force, *Z'A* goes through three prepatory states. First, from his original six *Sephirot* (infancy 1) he will get his higher four *Sephirot* which are his directive force, from ISOT 2 (growth 1). When these directive forces exit[58] it is infancy 2, when they come back to him through ISOT 1 (*Abah* and *Imah*), he has reached his full growth (growth 2).

---

[58] To get to his full growth, he needs to go through a second infancy

Therefore, for the two infancies and two growths of configuration *Z'A*, there are directive forces corresponding to each one of these different states of growth.

Directive forces of infancy

There are two types of directive forces of infancy: *Katnut* (infancy) 1 and *Katnut* 2.

When configuration *Z'A* only receives the *NHY (Netsa'h, Hod, and Yesod)* of his *Mo'hin* - interior - but not the encircling, they are the directive forces of *Katnut* 1.

When he receives the *NHY (Netsa'h, Hod, and Yesod)* of his directive forces directly from *Imah*, they are the directive forces of *Katnut* 2.

Directive forces of growth

There are two types of directive forces of *Gadlut* (growth): *Gadlut* 1 and *Gadlut* 2.

When configuration *Z'A* receives all his directive forces - interior and encircling from *ISOT,* they are directive forces of *Gadlut* 1. When he receives all his directive forces directly from *Imah*[59], they are directive forces of *Gadlut* 2, and he has now attained his full maturity.

---

[59] *NHY* of *Imah*

74

Face to Face

There is also a notion of closeness[60] and interaction, depending on whether the configurations face or turn their back to one another. The three possibilities are face to face, face to back, or back to back.

Face to face is the ideal level and corresponds to the bestowing of abundance.

When the configuration *Nukva* is ready for the *Zivug* (union), she comes face to face with the masculine; this is the ideal positioning for the union.

The guidance of the world is dependent on the different positioning and interactions of these masculine and feminine configurations, since they have a direct effect on the measure and balance of the factors of kindness, rigor and mercy.

Back to Face

Back to face is the second level. It is between the levels face to face, which is the ideal level that corresponds to the bestowing of abundance, and back to back, which corresponds to dissimulation and rigor.

---

[60] And readiness for the *Zivug* - union

75

Back to face denotes a readiness to get close from only one side. It is a position of waiting or longing for the ideal face to face situation.

Back to Back

Back to back is the lowest level and corresponds to dissimulation and rigor.

Back to back denotes an unreadiness to get close. It is a position that can not allow a union of the configurations for a bestowal or an action.

Zivug - Union

Once the configurations have received their respective directive forces and are in the face to face position, they are now ready for the *Zivug* - to unite.

Zivug is the union of the masculine with its feminine. All the outcomes of the higher emanations are a result of the different unions of the masculine and feminine lights.

There are different kinds[61] of *Zivugim* - unions:
- for the reparation of the worlds,
- for the building of the configurations
- for the guidance of the worlds.

---

[61] With different outcomes

For the reparation of the worlds

After the damage caused by the breaking of the vessels, reparation was needed to put in place the respective configurations in each world[62]. There was union of the *Sephirot* of *MaH (45)* and *BaN (52)* in complex arrangements, so as to allow the feminine *BaN (52)* to be repaired by the masculine *MaH (45),* and for the *Sephirot* to stand in the three-column arrangement of kindness, rigor and mercy.

For the building of the configurations

The union of a masculine and feminine configuration gives birth to a lower configuration. After the union, there is a period of gestation where the configuration is kept inside the superior feminine configuration to get his needed strength before coming out.

By the union of configuration *'Atik* and his *Nukva,* configurations *Arikh* and his *Nukva* were built, and from their union, *Abah* and *Imah* were built. By the union of configurations *Abah* and *Imah,* configurations *Z'A* and *Nukva* were built.

---

[62] In an organized order

For the guidance of the worlds

For configurations *Abah* and *Imah* there are two types of unions: the constant union is called exterior, and is for the subsistence of the worlds and no more; the other is called interior, and is for the renewing of the directive forces of configurations *Z'A* and *Nukva* for the guidance.

For the abundance to come down to the world, the masculine configuration *Zeir Anpin* needs to unite with *Nukva* - the feminine. There can be abundance only when the masculine and the feminine are in harmony. The guidance of the world is dependent on the different positioning and interactions of the masculine and feminine configurations, since they have a direct effect on the measure and balance of the factors of kindness, rigor and mercy.

The configurations of *Zeir Anpin* and *Nukva* are the root of all the created. It is by their unions and *Tikunim* - actions and inter-actions - that the guidance of justice is manifested. Each day, according to the actions of man, the prayers during the week, *Shabbat* or Holidays, and depending on time, various configurations allow different unions of configurations, resulting in outflows of abundance with variable intensities.

Two conditions are needed for the union to be possible: the configurations must be constructed, and the feminine must stimulate a reaction from the masculine[63].

All the abundance that descends to the world proceeds from the various unions of the masculine configurations *Zeir Anpin*, Israel, Ya'acov with the feminine configurations of *Nukva - Leah* or *Ra'hel*.

There are five different unions:

- The unions with *Ra'hel* are of the highest level, being of the aspect of kindness.
- The ones with *Leah* are more of the aspect of rigor.
- The one of *Israel* and *Ra'hel*[64] is the most superior. *Israel* represents all of *Z'A*, *Ra'hel* is the essential of *Nukva*. The abundance that is bestowed by this union is the most complete.
- The other unions of *Z'uN* are of different levels, at various times, and of lesser plenitude.

Each new day is of a new emanation that governs it. For each day, there are new unions of different aspects of *Z"uN* (*Zeir Anpin and Nukva*).

- In the *Tefilah* - prayer of *Sha'hrit*, there is the union of *Ya'acov* and *Ra'hel*[65]

---

[63] There is almost never an action from above without a stimulation from below
[64] *Musaf* of Shabat
[65] Also *'Arvit* of Shabat

- In the *Tefilah* of *Min'ha*, there is the union of *Israel* and *Leah*.
- In the *Tefilah* of *'Arvit*, there is the union of *Ya'acov* and *Leah* (from the chest up).
- In *Tikun 'Hatsot*, there is the union of *Ya'acov* and *Leah* (from the chest down).

The guidance of the world is strongly influenced by the different kinds of positioning and interactions of the configurations[66], since they emanate various intensities of kindness and rigor.

The goal of the service of the creatures is to help prepare the configurations *Z'A* and *Nukva* for the union, and this, as a result of the observance of the commandments and the different prayers. The prayers and the different Jewish rituals have hinted secret names and meditations that cause the elevation and adhesion of the worlds, and prepare the configurations for their unions.

---

[66] Their unions happen at different levels. They sometime ascend before joining

Chapter 6

WORLDS

A world is a possibility and a type of existence in a particular dimension. There are four worlds: Atsilut - the world of emanation, Beriah (creation) - the world of the Neshamot - souls, Yetsirah (formation) - the world of the angels and 'Asiah (action) - the physical world.

World - 'Olam

A world is a possibility and a type of existence in a particular dimension. From the first configuration; *Adam Kadmon* (*Primordial man*), emerged the emanations that made the other worlds[67].

There are four worlds. The first to unfold from *Adam Kadmon* is called *Atsilut,* the world of emanation, where there is no existence of the separated and no negative force even at its lowest levels.
The second world is *Beriah (creation)*, the world of the souls.
The third world is *Yetsirah (formation)*, the world of the angels.
The fourth world is *'Asiah (action)*, the world of physical existence

There is a screen (divider) that separates one world from another, and from this screen the ten *Sephirot* of the lower world emerge from the ten *Sephirot* of the higher world.

All the worlds are similar they each contain ten *Sephirot* and five main configurations: *See fig. 11*
- *Arikh Anpin*
- *Abah*
- *Imah*
- *Zeir Anpin*
- *Nukva*

---

[67] Four lower worlds

83

But the quintessence of the higher world is superior.

There is no interruption of the flowing of energies from both directions. All the worlds are joined by the last *Sephira* of the higher world which "connects" with the higher *Sephira* of the world under him. The three first *Sephirot* of configuration *'Atik Yomin* are in the *Sephira Malkhut* of the higher world, his seven lower *Sephirot* are in the first configuration *Arikh Anpin* of the world under it. *See fig. 12*

Over these four worlds, the four letters of the Name (י-ה-ו-ה) B'H govern.
י in *Atsilut;* by it, all the repaired levels are put in order.
ה descends from *Atsilut* to *Beriah* and guides it.
ו to *Yetsirah,*
ה to *'Asiah.*

Atsilut is of the aspect of configuration *Abah, Beriah* of *Imah, Yetsirah* of *Z'A,* and *'Asiah* of *Nukva.*

Atsilut – world of emanation

The first world[68], *Atsilut*, is the world of emanation, the world of divine thought. It is a completely spiritual world without any existence of separated entities. It brings into existence and sustains the other worlds. It is the highest of the four worlds, above *Beriah, Yetsirah* and *'Asiah.*

---

[68] After the world of *Adam Kadmon*

84

The first three *Sephirot* of his configuration *'Atik Yomin* are in the *Sephira Malkhut* of *Adam Kadmon*, while its seven lower *Sephirot* are inside the ten *Sephirot* of *Arikh Anpin* and make the link between *Atsilut* and *Adam Kadmon*.

From *Atsilut* unfolded all the lower worlds, which are the source of existence for the physical worlds and the possibility of reward, punishment and evil.

Beneath *Atsilut,* the lights of its *Malkhut* collided, and a curtain was made between *Atsilut* and *Beriah* from the striking of these lights. From there, other configurations similar to the ones in *Atsilut* were formed in the lower worlds, but of a lower force since the lights were dimmed by the curtain. It is because of the diminution of these light's intensities that existence for separated entities became possible.

The world of *Atsilut* is of the aspect of the name of *'A"V* and configuration *Abah.*

Atsilut

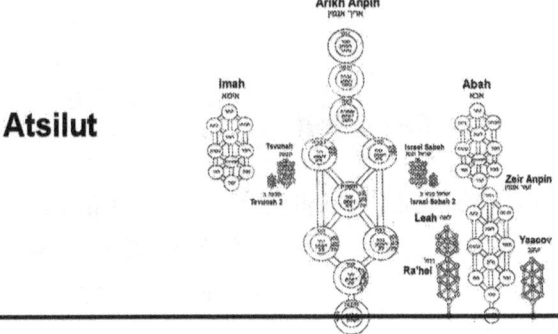

Fig. 11

Beriah – world of creation

The second world to unfold is called *Beriah*, the world of creation. It is the world of the souls. It is the first world where separate entities have the possibility of existence. These individual creations are of the highest spirituality; they are the souls with their full luminosity, before they descend into physical bodies[69]. *Beriah* is under *Atsilut* and above *Yetsirah* and *'Asiah*.

Beneath *Beriah,* under its curtain, other *Partsufim* similar to the ones in *Beriah* were formed in the lower world of *Yetsirah* - Formation, but of a lower force since the lights were even more dimmed by the curtain. It is because of the accrued diminution of the light's intensity that even more separated entities such as angels will come to be.

The world of *Beriah (Creation)* is of the aspect of the name of *SaG (63)*. Thus, *Beriah* is of the aspect of configuration *Imah* – *Sephira Binah*.

Yetsirah – world of formation

The third world to unfold is called *Yetsirah*; it is the world of formation, the world of the angels[70]. After *Beriah* which has separated entities, albeit of the highest spiritual level,

[69] And diminish from their original luminosity
[70] Their main world, some are also present in the other worlds

86

Yetsirah is also a spiritual world, but the angels that are its separated entities also have a spiritual form. This world is under *Atsilut* and *Beriah* but above *'Asiah*.

Beneath *Yetsirah,* under its curtain, other configurations similar to the ones in *Yetsirah* were formed in the lower world of *'Asiah* - Action. Because of the much-accrued diminution of the light's intensity, physical entities will be able to exist.

The world of *Yetsirah* is of the aspect of the name of *MaH* *(45)*. Thus, *Yetsirah* is of the aspect of configuration *Z'A*.

Angels

There are two types of angels: positive and negative. In the world of *Yetsirah* – formation, reside most of the different families of positive angels.

There are two kinds of positive angels: the angels of nature who were created at the beginning of the world: they are in charge of the nature itself. The second type[71] is the angels of "reward and punishment", They accomplish the divine will and are renewed constantly depending on the deeds of men.

The positive angels comprise ten groups and are divided as follows: three groups in the world of *Beriah* (Creation*)*, six groups in the world of *Yetsirah* (Formation)*,* and one group

---

[71] Subdivides in different categories

87

in the world of *'Asiah* (Action). Each group of angels has its own hierarchy and is divided into four camps: Michael, Gabriel, Uriel, and Raphael. There are also destructive angels in the lower worlds[72]; they subdivide into the same order as well. They consist of ten groups and are at the service of the lower negative force.

'Asiah – world of action

The fourth world to unfold is called *'Asiah* - Action, the world of physical existence. It is the furthest from the emanation of the light, which has now been filtered by the three worlds above it. All types of physical existence are now possible, and even the existence of opposite forces are allowed. It is the world of man as an entity composed of two contrary elements: a soul from the very high world of *Beriah*, and a physical body from the lower world of *'Asiah*. These two components are always in a condition of struggle, the soul being attracted and drawn to the realms of its spiritual origin, the body to this world's physical pleasures and vanities.

The world of *'Asiah* is of the aspect of the name of *BaN (52)*. Thus, *'Asiah* is of the aspect of configuration *Nukva – Sephira Malkhut*. From the last level of the *Sephirot* of *'Asiah* (*Malkhut* of *'Asiah*), the negative force emerged.

---

[72] *Beriah, Yetsirah and 'Asiah*

In parallel to the four worlds (*ABYA*), there are four types of existence in our world:

- mineral corresponding to *'Asiah (Action)*
- vegetal corresponding to *Yetsirah (Formation)*
- animal corresponding to *Beriah (Creation)*
- man corresponding to *Atsilut (Emanation)*

The other entity, which is called *Sitra A'hra* (the other side, or the negative force), has its own four worlds of *Atsilut*, *Beriah*, *Yetsirah* and *'Asiah*. It also has configurations, *Sephirot*, *Hekhalot* and angels, as in the positive world, but of a lower force.

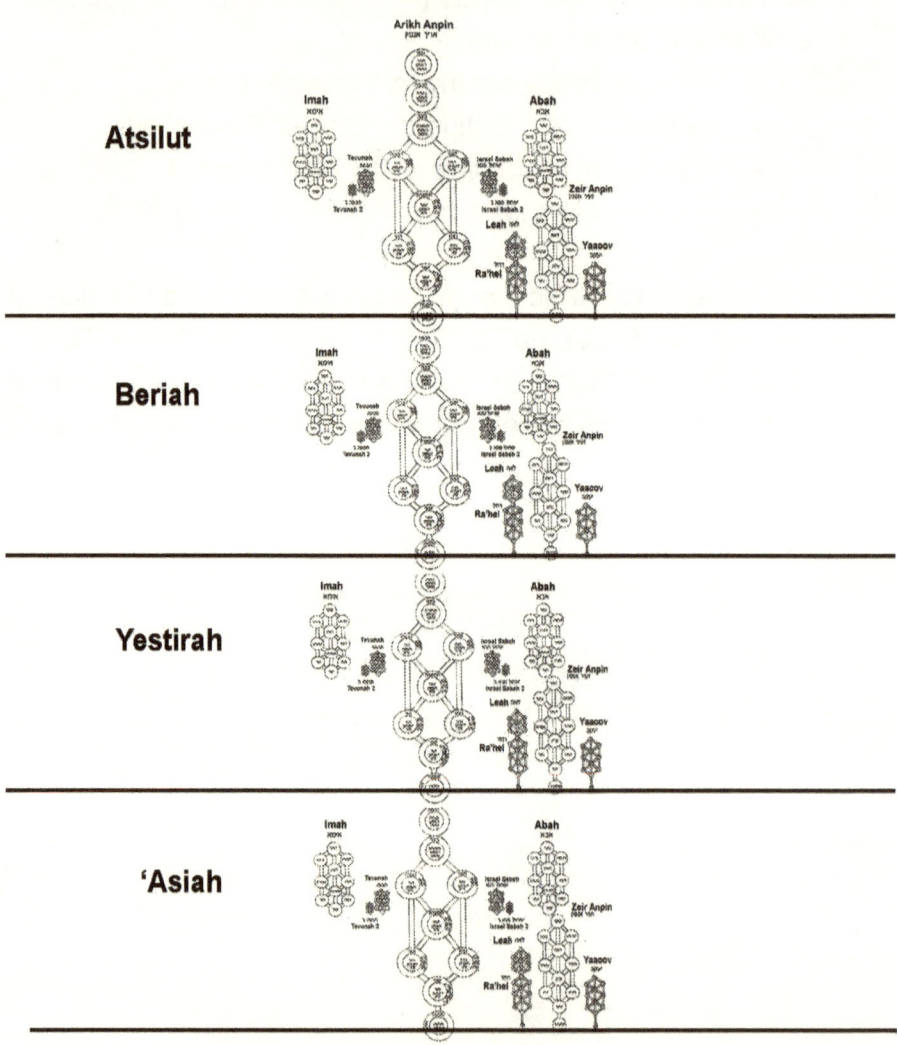

Fig. 12

90

Chapter 7

SOULS

The soul has five names: Nefesh, Rua'h, Neshama, 'Haya and Ye'hida, which correspond to its five levels. There are many divisions and categories of souls. They differ according to their origin or their level in the higher realms.

Five levels of the soul

The soul has five levels, their names are: *Nefesh*, *Rua'h*, *Neshama*, *'Haya* and *Ye'hida*. The soul is the spiritual entity inside the body, the latter being only its outer garment. Each soul has a precise root and a possibility of acquiring the highest level of this root[73]. All[74] come first with a lower level, and will, if they merit, attain the next higher level.

- *Nefesh* is the first and lower level. It is acquired at birth and before the succeeding levels. It corresponds to the level of the physical world of *'Asiah* and of the feminine configuration *Nukva*.

- *Rua'h* is the second level and is acquired before the succeeding levels. It corresponds to the level of the world of angels - *Yetsirah* and configuration *Zeir Anpin*.

- *Neshama* is the third level and can be acquired only after acquiring the level of *Nefesh* and *Rua'h*. It corresponds to the level of the world of souls - *Beriah* and configuration *Imah*.

- *'Haya* is the fourth level and can only be acquired after the preceding levels. It corresponds to the level of the world of emanation - *Atsilut* and configuration *Abah*.

---

[73] After reincarnations
[74] Men

93

- *Ye'hida* is the fifth and highest level; it is very rarely attained and can only be acquired after the *Tikun* (rectification) of all the preceding levels. It corresponds to the level of the world of emanation - *Atsilut* and configuration *Arikh Anpin*.

Soul	World	Configuration
Ye'hida	Atsilut	Arikh Anpin
Hayah	Atsilut	Abah
Neshama	Beriah	Imah
Rua'h	Yetsirah	Zeir Anpin
Nefesh	'Asiah	Nukva

Fig. 13: Correspondence between the five levels of souls, four worlds and five configurations

There are many divisions and categories of souls. They differ according to their origin or their level in the higher realms.

Each level of the soul is subdivided in five levels. As for the level of *Nefesh*, there are *Nefesh* of *Nefesh*, *Rua'h* of *Nefesh*, *Neshama* of *Nefesh*, *'Haya* of *Nefesh* and *Ye'hida* of *Nefesh*.

See fig. 14

Nefesh	Rua'h	Neshama	'Haya	Ye'hida
Ye'hida	Ye'hida	Ye'hida	Ye'hida	Ye'hida
'Haya	'Haya	'Haya	'Haya	'Haya (2)
Neshama	Neshama	Neshama	Neshama	Neshama
Rua'h	Rua'h	Rua'h	Rua'h	Rua'h
Nefesh (1)	Nefesh	Nefesh	Nefesh	Nefesh

Fig. 14: Each level of the soul has its own five levels

(1) *Nefesh* of *Nefesh* is the lowest level for a soul

(2) *'Haya* of *Ye'hida* is almost the highest

Level	Nefesh	Rua'h	Nesham	'Haya	Ye'hida
Nefesh	Ye'hida	Ye'hida	Ye'hida	Ye'hida	Ye'hida
Nefesh	'Haya	'Haya (1)	'Haya	'Haya	'Haya
Nefesh	Neshama	Neshama	Neshamä	Neshama	Neshama (3)
Nefesh	Rua'h (2)	Rua'h	Rua'h	Rua'h	Rua'h
Nefesh	Nefesh	Nefesh	Nefesh	Nefesh	Nefesh

Fig. 15: Each level of *Nefesh* subdivides again

Each level can again be subdivided, for example:
(1) *'Haya* of *Rua'h* of *Nefesh* is a higher level than
(2) *Rua'h* of *Nefesh* of *Nefesh* but lower than
(3) *Neshama* of *Ye'hida* of *Nefesh*

Each soul has its origin in the different worlds and configurations. The quality of the soul will depend on which configuration and from which world it has its root. A soul with a higher origin will be of superior quality and will have a better potential for understanding and approaching nearer to its

Creator, on the condition, of course, that it acts accordingly and reaches its potential.

Each one of these levels of the soul subdivides for each level of *Partsuf* - configuration and for each world. Therefore, there are five levels of soul for each configuration and there are five levels of configurations for each world, etc.

Soul / World	'Asiah	Yetsirah	Beriah	Atsilut	Atsilut
Ye'hida	Nukva (a)	Nukva	Nukva	Nukva	Nukva
'Haya	Nukva	Nukva	Nukva	Nukva (2)	Nukva
Neshama	Nukva	Nukva	Nukva	Nukva	Nukva
Rua'h	Nukva	Nukva	Nukva	Nukva	Nukva
Nefesh	Nukva (1)	Nukva (b)	Nukva	Nukva	Nukva

Fig.16: All possibilities of *Nukva* for the 5 levels of souls and worlds

(1) Soul of the level of Nefesh of Nukva of 'Asiah
(2) Soul of the level of 'Haya of Nukva of 'Atsilut

Ye'hida of Nukva of 'Asiah (a) is a lower level than Nefesh of Nukva of Yetsirah (b)

Each one of these levels can again subdivide in many, adding numerous possibilities[75].

Also, as there are ten *Sephirot* in each *Sephira*, world and *Partsuf*, the origin of a soul could be from one of the above subdivisions, subdivided again according to the ten *Sephirot*.

---

[75] Almost to the infinite

NEFESH	'Asiah	Yetsirah	Beriah	Atsilut	Atsilut
Keter	Nukva	Z'A	Imah	Abah	Arikh
'Hokhma	Nukva	Z'A	Imah	Abah	Arikh
Binah	Nukva	Z'A	Imah	Abah	Arikh
Da'at	Nukva	Z'A	Imah	Abah	Arikh
'Hesed	Nukva	Z'A	Imah (2)	Abah	Arikh
Gevurah	Nukva	Z'A	Imah	Abah	Arikh
Tiferet	Nukva (1)	Z'A	Imah	Abah	Arikh
Netsa'h	Nukva	Z'A	Imah	Abah	Arikh
Hod	Nukva	Zeir	Imah	Abah	Arikh
Yesod	Nukva	Zeir	Imah	Abah	Arikh
Malkhut	Nukva	Zeir	Imah	Abah	Arikh

Fig. 17: All the possibilities for *Nefesh* for the 10 *Sephirot* and 4 worlds

(1) Soul of the level of Tiferet of Nefesh of Nukva of 'Asiah

(2) Soul of the level of 'Hesed of Nefesh of Imah of Beriah

More divisions and subdivisions are possible, since each *Sephira* subdivides into ten almost indefinitely[76]. Each *Partsuf* - configuration also subdivides in ten *Sephirot* adding even more possibilities.

Since it is men that provoke the union of the *Sephirot* and *Partsufim* with their prayers and observation of the commandments, it is necessary for their souls to have their origin from them, each one according to his level.

---

[76] For this division of Nefesh, the same applies for each one of the five different levels of the soul

97

Sephira	Level of the soul		Tetragamon
Keter	Ye'hida	'	Extremity of Yud
'Hokhma	Hayah	'	Yud
Binah	Neshama	ה	First HeY
'Hesed	Rua'h	ו	Vav
Gevurah	Rua'h	ו	Vav
Tiferet	Rua'h	ו	Vav
Netsa'h	Rua'h	ו	Vav
Hod	Rua'h	ו	Vav
Yesod	Rua'h	ו	Vav
Malkhut	Nefesh	ה	Second HeY

Fig. 18

The goal of man is to reach each successively higher level of his soul; for that, he must perform the *Tikun* of the preceding levels. The higher levels of the soul cannot be acquired at once. Most men only have the level of *Nefesh*, and if they merit, they will acquire the succeeding levels - but one by one by dying and reincarnating. If he needs to acquire the level of *Imah* of *'Asiah*, first, he must perform the *Tikun* of *Malkhut* of *'Asiah*, *Z'A* of *'Asiah*, and so on. To acquire his level of *Neshama*, he must perform the *Tikun* of all the levels of the *Sephirot* and configurations of his *Nefesh* and *Rua'h, etc.*

To do this *Tikun* could take a few lifetimes, the soul will then reincarnate as many times as needed to accomplish it.

All these complex possibilities have only one purpose; to allow man to have merit by his own efforts and get closer to his Creator. For this, he must get a higher level of soul and elevate his ways by doing his own *Tikun*.

Chapter 8

REINCARNATION

The Gilgul is the reincarnation of a soul from the time of birth until death, the 'Ibur is an attachment of another soul to one's own, which could come and leave at anytime. When man makes his necessary Tikun, his soul can now rise to the higher realms and rejoin its source. But if man does not do the Tikun of the level of his soul for which he came, he comes back and reincarnates.

Reincarnation - Gilgul

To ascend from its original level, a soul needs to reincarnate[77] to do its *Tikun*. This *Tikun* of the soul is realized by the *Gilgul* (reincarnation) and/or by the *'Ibur* (attachment). While *Gilgul* is the reincarnation of a soul into a body from the time of its birth until its death, the *'Ibur* is an attachment of another soul to his own soul, that could come and leave at anytime.

If man does not do the *Tikun* for the level of his soul for which he came, he comes back and reincarnates in a new body for a new life. As long as he undertakes the *Tikun* of his soul in three reincarnations, he will come back again and again as needed, to complete his *Tikun*. However, if he maintains his wrong behavior[78] and neither performs nor advances in his *Tikun*, he will not return after the third reincarnation[79].

There are different reasons why a soul might have to come back and reincarnate. It could be to repair or rectify an act for some damage he caused by his wrongdoings, or by not accomplishing the *Mitsvot* – commandments. The secret and reasons behind the accomplishment of the *Mitsvot* is to help, or make the *Tikun* of the soul.

As there are 613 parts to the soul, and 613 veins and bones to man, similarly, there are 613 *Mitsvot* and 613 lights in

---

[77] As many times as needed
[78] In his three first reincarnations
[79] This soul will be destroyed

103

each *Sephira* or configuration. Each *Mitsva* corresponds to one part of the soul and of the body; by performing a positive commandment or avoiding a negative one, the corresponding part of the soul is reinforced and repaired. Failing to perform the positive *Mitsva* or to avoid a negative commandment causes direct damage to one's soul and requires repair in this life or in a future reincarnation.

It is only by getting another chance to do or undo what he should have done or not do, that man makes the necessary *Tikun* of his soul, which can now rise to the higher realms and rejoin its source.

There are different levels in a soul, and each one of them corresponds to a particular *Sephira*, configuration or world[80]. The systems for the *Tikun* of the souls are complex and follow a precise order of priority from the lowest to the highest level[81]. For its *Tikun*, a soul must first repair what is damaged or lacking in a lower level before moving to the next.

To reach the next higher level of his soul, man must completely perform the *Tikun* of the preceding level.

The five levels of the soul - *Nefesh, Rua'h, Neshama, 'Haya* and *Ye'hida* - correspond to the four worlds of *'Asiah, Yetsirah, Beriah* and *Atsilut.*

---

[80] Or a subdivision or combination of these
[81] See Sha'ar Hagilgulim from the Ari Z'al

REINCARNATION

Soul	World
Ye'hida	Atsilut
'Haya	Atsilut
Neshama	Beriah
Rua'h	Yetsirah
Nefesh	'Asiah

Fig. 19

To attain his level of *Rua'h*, which corresponds to *Yetsirah*[82], man must perform the *Tikun* of his *Nefesh*, corresponding to *'Asiah*.

For each world there are five levels of soul; therefore, each world subdivides again into five ascending levels. *See fig. 20*

Level	'Asiah	Yetsirah	Beriah	Atsilut
5	Ye'hida	Ye'hida	Ye'hida	Ye'hida
4	'Haya	'Haya	'Haya	'Haya
3	Neshama	Neshama	Neshama	Neshama
2	Rua'h	Rua'h	Rua'h	Rua'h
1	Nefesh	Nefesh	Nefesh(1)	Nefesh

Fig. 20

To get his first level of *Neshama*, which corresponds to *Nefesh* of *Beriah (1)*, man must perform the *Tikun* of all his levels of *Nefesh*, *Rua'h*, *Neshama*, *'Hayah* and *Ye'hidah* of the world of the worlds of *'Asiah* and *Yetsirah* as to repair

---

[82] They are both second levels

105

completely his levels of *Nefesh* and *Rua'h*, and to be able to get to his level of *Neshama*.

For each world there are also five levels of soul corresponding to the five *Partsufim*.

Level	'Asiah	Yetsirah	Beriah	Atsilut
5	Arikh Anpin	Arikh Anpin	Arikh Anpin (2)	Arikh Anpin
4	Abah	Abah	Abah	Abah
3	Imah	Imah	Imah	Imah
2	Z'A	Z'A	Z'A	Z'A
1	Nukva	Nukva	Nukva	Nukva

Fig. 21

To get his highest level of *Neshama*, which corresponds to *Arikh Anpin* of *Beriah (2)*, man must perform the *Tikun* of the five *Partsufim* of *'Asiah* and *Yetsirah* and the four first *Partsufim* of *Beriah*.

The five levels of the souls correspond also to the five configurations.

Soul	Configurations
Ye'hida	Arikh Anpin
'Haya	Abah
Neshama	Imah
Rua'h	Zeir Anpin
Nefesh	Nukva

106

The higher levels of the soul cannot be acquired at once. Most men only have the level of Nefesh[83]. If they merit, they will acquire or reincarnate to get the next levels - one by one.

In general, the level of Rua'h can not come before the age of thirteen, the level of Neshama at twenty, and the other levels afterwards.

It is possible to make the Tikun of all the levels in one lifetime. For that, all the levels have to be repaired one after the other in the same lifetime, and this has to be the first time that this soul has come into the world.

If man only makes the Tikun of his level of Nefesh[84], he will not get his Rua'h; he has to die first and come back to get it in his new life[85]. If he makes the Tikun of his Rua'h in his new life, he will not get his level of Neshama. He has to die again and then come back with his two levels of Nefesh and Rua'h to try to get his Neshama. Once these three levels are acquired, he does not need to reincarnate anymore[86].

Each Sephira corresponds to a level of soul

---

[83] Even after having come many lifetimes, they are still repairing the levels of Nefesh slowly and one by one
[84] All of its levels
[85] There is a limit of how much can be repaired in one single lifetime
[86] He has finished his Tikun and will return to his deserved place in the world of Beriah - creation

Sephira	Level of the soul
Keter	Ye'hida
'Hokhma	Hayah
Binah	Neshama
'Hesed	Rua'h
Gevurah	Rua'h
Tiferet	Rua'h
Netsa'h	Rua'h
Hod	Rua'h
Yesod	Rua'h
Malkhut	Nefesh

Each level of soul corresponds to one of the letters of the Name of G-od

Level of the soul	Tetragamon	
Ye'hida	'	Extremity of Yud
Hayah	'	Yud
Neshama	ה	First HeY
Rua'h	ו	Vav
Nefesh	ה	Second HeY

108

Attachment - 'Ibur

To help him make the *Tikun* of his soul, another soul may attach to his (*'Ibur*) to help him do the necessary repair or accomplish the missing *Mitsvot*. When he accomplishes this, the soul may stay longer or depart. The missing *Mitsva* could be one he chose not to do[87] or one he could not do in his previous life[88].

In general, the soul that attaches to him is of a higher and purer origin, from a family member, or from a *Tsadik*. As long as he does good deeds the soul could stay attached to his, but if he sins or makes the attached soul uncomfortable, it will depart.

There is a *Levush* (garment or envelope), which the soul needs to attach to the body of man (*Gilgul*), and when another soul attaches to him (*'Ibur*), it may use the same *Levush* to remain in him.

Sometimes the entire soul does not need to come back; instead, only the parts that need to be repaired (by doing the missing *Mitsva*) come again. Or, different parts of one soul may reincarnate in more than one person in the same life time to perform the *Tikun*.

---

[87] He had the possibility to accomplish it but did not
[88] He did not have the possibility to accomplish it, as the *Mitsva* of circumcision if he did not have a son etc.

109

There are four types of existence in our world:

- mineral corresponding to *'Asiah (Action)*
- vegetal corresponding to *Yetsirah (Formation)*
- animal corresponding to *Beriah (Creation)*
- man corresponding to *Atsilut (Emanation)*

Man could reincarnate in one of these four types of existence, mineral being the harshest punishment because of its incapacity to act. But generally, in order to make his *Tikun*, he will not reincarnate in a mineral, vegetal and rarely in an animal.

The goal of all these complex systems of reincarnation has only one purpose: to give man a possiblily to surpass his main limitation which is time, by coming again and again to do the *Tikun* of his soul and merit a better place in the *'Olam Haemet* - world of truth.

Chapter 9

GUIDANCE

The will of the Creator is to bestow goodness on His creatures; all the levels of creation were put in place so His kindness could fully emanate to them. The guidance of the worlds is done through the influence of the different Sephirot and Partsufim (configurations).

Guidance

At first[89], the Creator was alone, filling all space with His energy. He was not bestowing His influence because there was no one to receive it. When He willed to create, He started to influence. Kabbalah is the only science that, in the least details, explains to us the true guidance[90] of the world, so that we may understand His will.

The will of the Creator is to bestow goodness on His creatures; all the levels of creation and their guidance were put in place so His kindness could emanate to them, yet in such a way that they would be able to receive it.

The light of G-od is unique, of equal force, quality and beyond all description. The guidance of the world is manifested by different types of attributes such as rigor, mercy, etc. This unique light is therefore transformed or filtered by other lights, to give it various qualities or forces for a guidance based on the system of free choice, punishment, and reward.

These "transforming", secondary lights are called *Sephirot* or *Partsufim* - configurations, and also attributes or qualities of G-od. A *Sephira* is, in a way, a "filter" that when the unique light enters it, transforms it into a particular force or quality by which the Creator guides the worlds.

---

[89] The science of Kabbalah only starts after the first act of this creation which is the *Tsimtsum*

[90] By describing all the emanations of His energies, their transformations through the *Sephirot* and their multiple and complex actions

113

The Kabbalah explains to us very precisely this true guidance, and how the worlds are guided by these extremely complex systems of forces or lights, which through their interactions provoke chain reactions that impact directly upon man and the worlds. Each one of these reactions has numerous ramifications with many details and results.

This complex system of forces or lights are the different *Tikunim* (actions) and *Zivugim* (unions) of the *Sephirot* and configurations to influence and make the guidance by means of their different arrangements and amalgamations.

There are two main kinds of guidance:
 - The general guidance, which is for the subsistence of the worlds, and is not influenced by the actions of men.

This guidance is by means of the encircling *Sephirot*.

 -    The variable guidance, which is on the basis of justice, reward and punishment and is dependant on time and on the actions of man.

This guidance is by the linear *Sephirot* that are arranged in three columns: right, left and middle, representing the guidance of the world in the manner of kindness, rigor and mercy. *See fig. 25*

Rigor   Mercy   Kindness

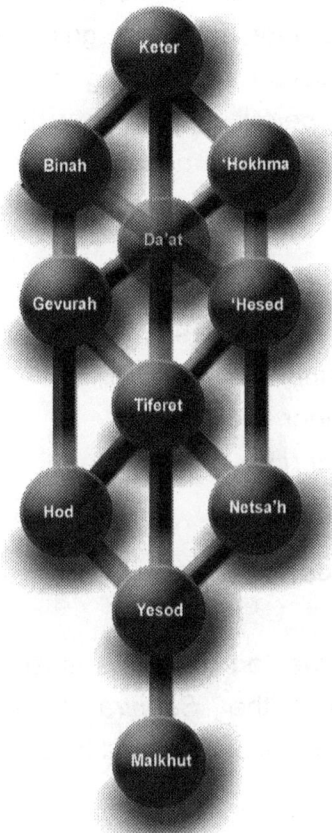

Fig. 25

The guidance is mostly influenced by the different positioning and interactions of the masculine and feminine configurations, since they have a direct effect on the measure and balance of the factors of kindness, rigor and mercy.

The masculine configurations bestow kindness, the feminine bestow rigor. By their union, different equilibriums of the two forces of kindness and rigor make the guidance. Complete rigor will be the destruction of anything not perfect, while complete kindness will permit everything without restriction. However, these two aspects are necessary for the guidance based on justice, and for giving man the possibility of free choice.

The guidance is manifested by three main attributes:
- the attribute of kindness – right pillar
- the attribute of rigor – left pillar
- the attribute of mercy – middle pillar

The attribute of kindness

Kindness is mostly manifested by all the masculine aspects of the configurations[91], the Sephira 'Hesed, by the concealments of the aspects of rigor and by the illuminations of the higher lights.

There are special moments, or days of bounty during the year, such as the Shabbat and Holidays. This is dependent on the different positions of the configurations[92]. When the masculine and feminine configurations are face to face, it is the ideal level and corresponds to the bestowing of

---

[91] Aspects of the name of MaH – (45)
[92] It is because of the positions of these configurations every year at the same time, that these days are special

116

abundance[93]. In the attribute of bounty, the guidance is from the right pillar – the pillar of kindness.

The attribute of judgment

Rigor is mostly manifested by all the feminine aspects as: the name of *BaN (52)*, the *Sephira Gevurah* and by all the concealments of the masculine aspects that represent bounty.

There are particular moments, or days of rigor during the year[94]. This is dependent on the different positions of the configurations. In the absence of *Zivug* (union), when the masculine and feminine configurations are back to back, it corresponds to dissimulation and rigor. In the attribute of judgment, the guidance is from the left pillar – the pillar of rigor.

The attribute of mercy

In the attribute of mercy, the guidance is from the middle pillar – the pillar of mercy. This attribute makes the balance between the attributes of rigor and bounty, to allow a more equilibrated guidance for the present existence. Without this equilibrium there would not be a possibility of guidance based on merit – reward and punishment, also called guidance of justice.

---

[93] Face to face allows a possibility of *Zivug* - union
[94] As the days of fasting

Will

All the Kabbalists agree that it is not possible to understand or have the slightest notion of the Nature of G-od, since our comprehension cannot attain this level[95]. However, by understanding these systems of guidance, we can learn to understand His will, how and why He created the world in what way He directs it, the purpose of the existence of evil, and the reasons for the dualism of reward and punishment, etc.

It is by understanding His will that we realize the importance of man, because only he, by getting closer to the Creator and observing His commandments, can influence these incredible forces that impact directly upon the guidance of the worlds.

Will to bestow

The will of the Creator is to bestow only goodness on His creatures, and to bring all the creation to participate in the revelation of His unicity at the end of the six thousand years. It is to give men the possibility of merit that His bounty is not revealed openly and that manifestations of the aspects of rigor are put in force.

There is no existence that is not composed of the aspects of the name of *MaH* (45) or *BaN* (52); the influencer and the

---

[95] But we can and are allowed to learn to understand His will from the time of creation

118

receiver, the masculine and the feminine, bounty and rigor etc. The *Ein Sof*, B'H, influences when there is instigation from the receiver, the latter corresponding to the feminine receiving aspect of *BaN* (52). This influence is transmitted by the different illuminations of the *Sephirot* and then to the worlds.

It is the different equilibriums of the two forces of kindness and rigor that make the guidance. When rigors dominate harshness prevails, when bounty is in force, peace and kindness are bestowed. Thus, we see that everything that is, and happens, is always composed of a variable measure and balance of these two forces.

By allowing man to merit by his own efforts to get closer[96] to his Creator and receive His goodness, we see a very clear demonstration of His perfect justice.

Will to receive

By his nature man is himself a *Keli* (recipient) with a will to receive without limits, and containing a spiritual light; his soul. A guidance based on this desire of only receiving will not allow man to merit by his own efforts to get closer to his Creator.

These dual, attractive forces of good and bad influence man's choices and the ways or levels of his service to the

---

[96] By observing His commandments and by praying

119

Creator. It is by his own free choice that he will choose his way and control these contrary forces.

The perfect goal for man is to elevate his bodily desires by sanctifying his ways, and resembling his Creator, by becoming a giver with a will to bestow goodness to all.

Free choice

The two main aspects of the present guidance, which are kindness and justice, were put in place to give man the possibility of serving the Creator by his free will.

At the creation, when the breaking of the seven *Sephirot* caused an important damage, G-od emanated lights of the aspect of the name of *MaH (45)* to repair the deterioration that was caused by this unbalanced inflow of energies. He could have done the complete *Tikun* (repair) of all the worlds with one emanation, but then, there would not have been a reason for the participation of man in this *Tikun*.

To give man the possibility of acting upon and repairing creation, G-od in a way, restrained His outflow of kindness to this world, to allow men to have merit by making the *Tikun*[97] with their own free will. While man's good deeds have an effect on the four higher worlds, his bad deeds have consequences upon the four lower worlds. It is only when man sins that the negative side can grow in strength. The

---

[97] Bring back up the fallen sparks

root of the *Sitra A'hra* (negative force) is in the lack or absence of the *Kedushah* (holiness). Its existence was willed by the Creator to also give man free choice.

The good and bad impulse

These forces of good and bad, positive and negative, are in a constant battle at the level of the world of *'Asiah* (our physical world). Inside of man, these forces are: *Yetser Hatov* corresponding to his good or positive impulse and *Yetser Hara'* corresponding to his bad or negative impulse.

This negative aspect (his *Yetser Hara'*) grows inside of man, cuts him off from the higher worlds, and uproots him from the *Kedushah* - holiness. It almost constantly tries to seduce him and make him stumble, while the *Yetser Hatov* (positive aspect), on the other side, tries to attract him to *Torah* and *Mitsvot* and to help him do the *Tikun* of his *Neshama*.

Without these two aspects of *Yetser Tov* and *Yetser Hara'*, men would be like angels, with no power to decide either on their actions or on their service to the Creator. Therefore, they would gain no merit from choosing good over bad, or following His commandments.

Free choice also gives rise to a system of perfect justice, whereby men will be punished or recompensed according to their own decisions and free choice.

121

The names of G-od

The forces or energies that make or influence the guidance are also identified or described as the different names of G-od. *See fig. 26*

The main names are:
- Y-H-V-H - ה-ו-ה-י
- Ein Sof - אין סוף
- Adona-y - י -אדנ
- Ahy-h - אהי-ה
- Elohi-M - אלוה-ים

Sephira	Name	
Keter	אהי-ה	AHY-H
'Hokhma	ה-י	YH
Binah	י-ה-ו-ה	YHV-H (vowels of Elohi-m)
Da'at	אהו-ה	AHV-H
'Hesed	אל	EL
Gevurah	אלהי-ם	Elohi-m
Tiferet	י-ה-ו-ה	YHV-H
Netsa'h	יהו-ה -צבאות	YKVK Tsebaot
Hod	אלהי-ם צבאות	Elohi-m Tsebaot
Yesod	שד- י	Shada- y
Malkhut	אדנ- י	Adona- y

Fig. 26

Ein Sof

Ein Sof – The without limit or Infinite, is the most used Name for G-od in the Kabbalah. Since His light or energy cannot be measured by any definition or limiting terms, we therefore use the name "*Ein Sof*" (without limit) since we know and admit that G-od and the concept of limitlessness or without end is beyond our human comprehension. This name represents kindness.

Adona-y

This name represents the feminine aspect of G-od; it has an aspect of rigor and is represented by the *Sephira Malkhut*. It also represents the feminine configurations of *Ra'hel* and *Leah*. Since men's prayers are first directed to the *Sephira Malkhut* before they can be transmitted higher, this name also represents the closest relationship between man and his Creator.

Ahy-h

This name represents the higher masculine aspect of G-od, and is represented by the *Sephira Keter*. It shows kindness together with the awe of G-od.

Elohi-M

One of the names of G-od, represented by the *Sephira Gevurah*. In general, it denotes rigor in the actions of G-od.

Y-H-V-H (י-ה-ו-ה)

The primary name of G-od reveals kindness and mercy, represented by the *Sephira Tiferet*. All that was created has its origin in these four letters. Most of the guidance is manifested by this name and its different spellings that make new individual names.

By spelling each one of the four letters of this name differently, the numerical value of the name changes, and each one of these possibilities becomes different in its nature and actions.

בן	BaN	52
מה	MaH	45
סג	SaG	63
עב	A"V	72

The four *Miluyim* (spellings) are:

		ה	ו	ה	י		
'A'V	עב	הי	ויו	הי	יוד		
		15	22	15	20	=	72
SaG	סג	הי	ואו	הי	יוד		
		15	13	15	20	=	63
MaH	מה	הא	ואו	הא	יוד		
		6	13	6	20	=	45
BaN	בן	הה	וו	הה	יוד		
		10	12	10	20	=	52

Each name can also be divided and subdivided to describe even more precisely the different outcomes and manifestations of these energies:

'A"V of 'A"V, SaG of 'A"V, MaH of 'A"V ...
BaN of BaN of SaG, SaG of MaH of 'A"V etc.

The lights or forces that are clothed in these letters or their combinations emanate masculine or feminine configurations that make the guidance of the worlds.

Chapter 10

PRAYER

The order of the Tefilot – prayers – is based on the systems of ascension of the worlds, as explained in the Kabbalah. At this level, we understand that our prayers *have a direct influence on the superior worlds and on their guidance. When one understands the systems and actions of the* prayers, *he realizes the importance of our rituals, because only man, by praying and performing the Mitsvot, can influence these incredible forces.*

Tefilah - Prayer

The order of the prayers is based on the systems of ascension of the worlds, as explained in the Kabbalah. The purpose of this ascension of the worlds is to provoke a union between the masculine and feminine configurations, that they might bestow positive energies as a result of this harmony. At this level of comprehension, we understand that our prayers have a direct influence on the superior worlds, and on their guidance.

Beginning with the first act of the morning of *Netilat Yadayim* (washing of the hands three times in alternation), until the end of the *Tefilah*[98], there is a constant elevation and adhesion of the worlds of *'Asiah* (action), *Yetsirah (formation)* and *Beriah (creation)* to the fourth highest world of *Atsilut (emanation)*. This is done by the *Hekhalot* (portals); they are the different levels of ascension of the prayers before reaching the world of *Atsilut* during the *'Amidah.* Their principal function is to allow the adhesion and attachment of these worlds in a precise order.

During the prayers, when one knows this system of ascension of the *Hekhalot,* he concentrates on the words or the names, by which is hinted the precise action of the *Hekhal (portal)* that makes this ascension. *See fig. 28*

---

[98] *Sha'hrit* - Prayer of the morning

129

To get from one world to the next, a secret name called *MaV* (42), which is hinted at during the *Kadish*, makes this ascension possible. This secret name of 42 letters is made with the four letters of the name י-ה-ו-ה, the *Miluy* (spelling) of each one of the four letters for a total of ten letters, and the *Miluy* of each one of these ten letters for a total of twenty eight. This name is hinted when we answer *Yehe Sheme* ..... until - *Be'alma*. The *Kadish* makes possible the ascent of each world to the next higher world and the descent afterwards from the world of *Atsilut* to *'Asiah*.

	Hekhal / Portal	**Corresponding to**
First	לבנת הספיר (*Livnat Hasapir*)	*Yesod* and *Malkhut*
Second	עצם השמים (*Etsem Hashamayim*)	*Hod*
Third	נוגה (*Nogah*)	*Netsa'h*
Fourth	זכות (*Zekhut*)	*Gevurah*
Fifth	אהבה (*Ahavah*)	*'Hesed*
Sixth	רצון (*Ratson*)	*Tiferet*
Seventh	קדש קדשים (*Kodesh Kodashim*)	*Keter, 'Hokhma, Binah*

Fig. 28

130

The goal of all the prayers is to help prepare the different masculine and feminine configurations[99] for their *Zivug (union)*. It is only once they are united that our *"Avodah"* (work - duty) is done, and because of this higher harmony we can now receive from above.

There can be abundance only when the masculine and the feminine are in full harmony. Each day, according to the actions of man, the prayers during the week, *Shabbat* or Holidays, and depending on time, various configurations allow different[100] *Zivugim* (unions), and therefore outflows of abundance of variable intensities.

Each new day is of a new emanation that governs it. For each day, there are new configurations of different aspects of the masculine configuration *Z'A* and his feminine *Nukva*.

A full day is divided in two: day and night; and each half is again divided in two (dawn and day, dusk and night[101]). For each part, there is a prayer, for the two parts of day - *Sha'hrit* and *Min'ha*, and for the two parts of nights - *'Arvit* and *Tikun 'Hatsot*[102].

Generally, the *Zivugim* - unions of the configurations are:

---

[99] Masculine configurations of *Z'A* or *Ya'acov* with the feminine configurations of *Ra'hel* or *Leah*
[100] Different in their place of *Zivug* also
[101] Middle of the night
[102] *'Hatsot* means half. From the rising of the sun to the sunset divided by two, we add twelve hours to get to the "middle" of the night.

- *Sha'hrit*[103] - configurations *Ya'acov* and *Ra'hel*
- *Min'ha*[104] – configurations *Israel* and *Leah*
- *'Arvit*[105] – configurations *Ya'acov* and *Leah* (from the chest up)
- *Tikun 'Hatsot*[106] – configurations *Ya'acov* and *Leah* (from the chest down)
- The union of configurations *Israel* and *Ra'hel* is realized during the prayer of *Musaf* on *Shabbat* and on other special occasions.

When one understands the systems and actions of the prayers, he realizes the importance of our rituals, because man by praying, acts directly on these incredible forces.

Kavanah - concentration

To reach a more active role in the unification of the different configurations, one needs to understand and concentrate when praying. There are different levels of *Kavanah* - concentration. The basic *Kavanah* is to understand the words, and concentrate on the intention of the blessing or the prayer. The higher level is to meditate on the different systems of permutation of names and configurations, to get a particular action or result. Each word or part of the prayers has its own action or purpose. These actions are initiated by

---

[103] Prayer of the morning
[104] Prayer of the afternoon
[105] Prayer of the evening
[106] Prayer of the middle of the night

concentrating on the different names of G-od, their appellations and other arrangements of the *Autiot* – letters[107].

When saying a blessing with the Kabbalistic meditation on the appropriate words or names, we act and participate directly on the *Tikun* - rectification of the action or thing being blessed. The purpose of most of the blessings recited before and after eating or drinking is to liberate the souls that have been reincarnated in these comestible elements.

When praying, it is important to be part of a *Minyan* – a group with a minimum of ten men. Without this minimum number, the *Kadish* and other important parts of the prayer cannot be recited. For the morning prayer, one also has to wear a *Talit* – praying shawl, and *Tefilin* – phylacteries wrapped on the head and left arm.

Tefilin - Talit

Phylacteries - praying shawl

Since the goal is to make the upper masculine and feminine energies unite, man has to "resemble" physically the higher masculine configuration, i.e. configuration *Zeir Anpin*. The *Tefilin* on the head represent the directive lights he receives from the higher configuration of *Imah*; the *Tefilin* on the hand represent the feminine configuration that attaches to his left side. The *Talit* represents his surrounding lights given also by the configuration *Imah*.

---

[107] As explained by the Ari Z'al in his book *Sha'ar Hakavanot*

133

After configuration *Zeir Anpin* receives his directive lights from the higher configuration of *Imah* and they enter his head, they emerge from his forehead toward the outside in four different lights. The *Tefilin* of the head represent these lights; they comprise four compartments, each one containing a portion of text from the Torah, written on parchment.

Each one of these four lights also brings out an aspect of *Levush* (garment), which are the four compartments for the *Parashiot.*

Since the *Mo'hin* are directive lights that comprise ten *Sephirot,* the *Tefilin* are a representation of these ten lights:

The four compartments on the forehead are the *Sephirot HBD* - *'Hokhma, Binah, Da'at* (which divides in two).

The two straps on the side of the head are the *Sephirot 'Hesed* and *Gevurah.*

The knot on the back is *Sephira Tiferet.*

The two straps that come down on the sides are the *Sephirot Netsa'h* and *Hod: Netsa'h* until the chest and *Hod* until the navel.

The knot that makes the ' *(Yud)* on the *Tefilin* of the hand is the *Sephira Yesod* of configuration *Z'A*. From there (the arm of *Z'A*), the building of the feminine configuration begins.

The *Tefilin* on the arm represent the feminine configuration *Ra'hel*. The order of the *Parashiot* is the same as in the *Tefilin* on the head, but in only one parchment.

The three wrappings on the biceps correspond to the three first *Sephirot* of *Nukva*. The seven wrappings on the forearm correspond to the seven lower *Sephirot*.

The three wrappings on the finger correspond to the *NHY* *(Netsa'h, Hod, and Yesod)* of *Z'A*, which enter inside the *Nukva* to be its *Mo'hin* - directive lights.

Since configuration *Z'A* receives two types of directive lights, one from the configuration *Abah*, and one from the configuration *Imah*, there are two types of *Tefilin:*

- *Tefilin* of *Imah* are called *Tefilin* of *Rashi*. They are the regular type worn by all
- *Tefilin* of *Abah* are called *Tefilin* of *Rabenu Tam*. They are worn by only a few, together or after the ones of *Rashi*

The difference is in the order of the writing of the four Torah portions – *Parashiot*.

As we can see, every element of the prayers, whether physical or spiritual, has very deep and essential meanings to

135

give important forces and power to the one praying. It is a pity that these powerful and beautiful rituals are taken mistakenly for "folkloric recitations" in an incomprehensible language, part of "one has to do" type of thing when attending a prayer in a synagogue.

By making the effort to understand the deeper meanings of these rituals, one will discover a whole new definition and reason for his special relationship with the higher worlds and his Creator

Chapter 11

NEGATIVE FORCE

There is a "second" authority called Sitra A'hra - negative force, or "evil". Its husks obstruct the lights of the Sephirot, conceal man from his root and from the light. The Sephirot have their root in the holiness of the Ein Sof; the root of the negative force is in the lack, or absence of this holiness. Because of the bad deeds of the lower beings, the negative husks get their strength and do harm and evil in the world by attaching to the higher lights.

Evil – Sitra A'hra

There is a "second" authority called *Sitra A'hra*[108] - negative force or "evil". Even though it is the opposite of everything good, it is important to understand that the origin of "evil" is from an emanation of the superior lights[109], and thus, it does not really have a complete independent authority. It nourishes itself from the lower extremities of the holiness, and needs permission to act from above.

There is really only <u>one</u> unique and full authority, and it is the one of the Creator.

At the creation, when the ten feminine *Sephirot* of the aspect of the name of *BaN (52)* came out from the eyes of *Adam Kadmon*, the first three *Sephirot* – *KHB (Keter, 'Hokhma, Binah)* – were able to stand in the three column arrangement. However, the seven lower *Sephirot* did not stand in this order; they were not able to retain their lights and consequently broke. This was the first imperfection or damage in the creation. It is only when there are three columns, where the one of mercy stands between the columns of kindness and rigor that the three can attach and bind together for a harmonious balance.

---

[108] "Other side" in Aramaic
[109] Since everything originates from the *Kav* and *Rechimu*

139

This imperfect arrangement is the first origin of the negative force or "evil". This type of existence could not come to be from a perfect source; it had to originate from a defective state.

The breaking of the seven lower *Sephirot* caused a descent of all the worlds. The world of *'Asiah* fell even lower and from its end[110], the negative force emerged.

The *Sephirot* have their root in the holiness of the *Ein Sof*, *B'H*. The root of the negative force is in the lack or absence of the holiness. These husks obstruct the lights of the *Sephirot*, concealing man from his root and from the light.

In parallel (opposite) to the four worlds, this negative entity has its own four worlds, where ten groups of negative angels divide as follows:

- three groups in their world of *Beriah*
- six groups in their world of *Yetsirah*
- one group in their world of *'Asiah*.

They nourish from the extremities of the higher lights when the latter are weakened by the bad deeds of the lower beings. When this negative force receives its strength by sucking on these higher lights, its destructive angels get more powers and come to do evil in the world.

---

[110] *Malkhut* of *'Asiah*

The existence of the *Sitra A'hra* - negative force - was willed by the Creator to give man free will. With falsehood, it almost constantly tries to seduce him, and make him stumble.

The good deeds of man have an effect on the four higher worlds, his bad deeds on the four lower worlds. It is only when man sins that the negative side can grow in strength[111].

When man acts negatively, he attracts a derivative of this negative force that grows inside him. This is his *Yetser Hara';* it cuts him off from the higher worlds and the holiness. When he acts positively, he attracts positive energies that weaken the negative energies inside of him and give him strength to come closer to its creator.

Husks – Klipot

The husks are the individual manifestations of the negative force. They obstruct the lights of the lower *Sephirot* by attaching and nurturing from their extremities. They conceal man from the truth and from the light. Because of the bad deeds of the lower beings, the husks get and renew their strength to do evil in the world.

The *Tikunim* (rectifications) of the lower beings consist in detaching these husks from the holiness, by accomplishing the commandments and by the prayers. When men act negatively, they produce contrary energies that cause

---

[111] And vice-versa

141

deteriorations that reach the lower worlds and create even more husks to do harm.

There are four main levels of husks, they correspond to the four lower worlds. They too comprise *Sephirot* and configurations as in the positive worlds, and are also built on the three column arrangement of the *Sephirotic* trees. But they have the aim of acting contrary to the above positive worlds by emanating negative and hurtful energies.

Chapter 12

TIKUN

In Hebrew, the word "Tikun" has different meanings. It can be understood as reparation and also as relation or action. There are different types of Tikunim: to repair the worlds, for the construction and inter-relations of the Sephirot and configurations, for the guidance of the world and for the rectification of the souls.

Tikun
Rectification or action

Tikun in the Kabbalah is a very important notion. It shows, in a way, that everything that was created with a possibility of deficiency also has a potential to be rectified[112]. In Hebrew, the word "*Tikun*" has different meanings; it can be understood as reparation or rectification but also as function, relation or action.

There are different types of *Tikunim*:

- *Tikunim* (reparations) that took place in the first emanations to repair the worlds.
- *Tikunim* (rectifications - relations) for the construction and inter-relations of the *Sephirot* and configurations.
- *Tikunim* (actions - functions) of certain configurations for the guidance of the world.
- *Tikunim* (rectifications) for the *souls*.

Tikunim (reparations) to repair the worlds

At the creation, when from the configuration of *Adam Kadmon* emerged the ten *Sephirot* of the feminine aspect of *BaN* (52), and the seven lower *Sephirot* broke. To sustain the recipients of these *Sephirot* after they broke, 288 sparks of their lights came down as well to keep them alive.

---

[112] By man

This important damage - *Shvirat HaKelim* – the breaking of the vessels needed to be repaired. A first *Tikun* was to help in the ascent of some of these fallen 288 sparks, and to repair the recipients that had broken when they fell, that they might return to their respective lights.

The *Tikun* to repair the *Sephirot* after this damage was the union of the masculine *Sephirot* of *MaH (45)* with the feminine *Sephirot* of *BaN (52)* in complex arrangements. This was in order to allow the feminine *BaN* to be repaired[113] by the masculine *MaH,* and for the *Sephirot* to stand in the three-column arrangement for the guidance of kindness, rigor and mercy.

Tikunim (rectifications - relations) for the construction of the configurations

The *Tikunim* for the construction of the *Partsufim* - configurations are achieved by way of *Zivug* (union) of the higher masculine and feminine configurations, during which time the lower configuration will go through a period of gestation inside the feminine higher configuration, followed by its birth.

The masculine corresponds to *'Hesed* - kindness - and the name of *MaH (45)*, the feminine to *Gevurah* - rigor and the name of *BaN (52)*.

---

[113] But not completely

At first, during the period of gestation when the lower configuration is inside the upper *Nukva* (the feminine configuration above), the feminine and masculine lights of the aspect of *BaN* and *MaH* build and give the strength needed for the birth of the lower configuration. It is only when completely arranged and completed, that it is revealed[114]. There is afterwards a period of suckling, and then a first and second infancy and growth.

Tikunim (rectifications - relations) of the configurations for the guidance

There are also *Tikunim* of different configurations which are their actions, illuminations, and inter-relations in order to influence the guidance of the worlds. These *Tikunim* result in various illuminations of different intensities, depending on time and the actions of man.

The main *Tikunim* of the configurations are those of configurations *Arikh Anpin, Zeir Anpin,* and *Nukva.* Allegorically, these *Tikunim* are from the head, or the face of the configurations.

Tikunim of configuration Arikh Anpin

The first and highest *Tikun* is the one of the three first *Sephirot* of configuration *Arikh Anpin.*

---

[114] Outside as an independent configuration

147

These three *Sephirot* are the roots of the direction of kindness, rigor and mercy. To influence the guidance, illuminations are projected from one or more of these *Sephirot* to the configurations *Abah* and *Imah,* and from there, to the *Mo'hin* (directive force) of the configuration *Zeir Anpin.*

Lights arise from one of these *Sephirot* − *'Hokhma,* they spread downward and divide into thirteen. They are called the thirteen *Tikunim* of the *Dikna* - beard of *Arikh Anpin.*

The other *Tikunim* - illuminations of configuration *Arikh Anpin* are lights needed for the attainment and abundance. However, the guidance itself is from the lights that emanate from his *Dikna* − beard.

Tikunim of configuration Zeir Anpin

The higher emanations of lights are transmitted in a set order to the lower configurations. They finally come to configuration *Z'A* which, after emanating his own, will unite with the feminine configurations of Ra'hel or Leah, and transmit through them these emanations to the worlds, to make the guidance.

For configuration *Z'A* the *Tikunim* are expressed by the lights that come out of him, such as the hair - illuminations on his head, and on his face.

148

These emanations are called hair or beard because they are lights that spread out in individual conduits.

These *Tikunim* - actions are similar to the ones of configuration *Arikh Anpin,* but with some differences, they are more of the aspect of *Gevurah,* while those of *Arikh Anpin* express bounty. Nine at first, they become thirteen and act as a principle of kindness for the guidance of justice.

Tikunim (rectifications) for the souls

A *Tikun* for a soul is its rectification because of its unfulfillment or to cleanse it from any defect. The *Tikun* for the soul is realized by the *Gilgul* (reincarnation) and by the *'Ibur* (attachment). By accomplishing what he did not complete of the 613 *Mitsvot,* by rectifying an act or a damage he caused by his wrongdoings, man makes the necessary *Tikun* of his soul, which can now ascend to the higher realms and rejoin its source.

There are different types of *Tikunim* – rectifications for the soul, each one of its levels[115] needs its own *Tikun.* Most men only have the lower level of *Nefesh,* and if they do the proper *Tikun,* they will acquire the succeeding levels[116] - albeit one by one. A *Tikun* of a higher level can only be accomplished after all the preceding levels.

---

[115] Five levels of the soul
[116] After reincarnating again

149

As long as one undertakes the *Tikun* of his soul within three reincarnations, he will reincarnate and return as needed to complete his *Tikun*. However, if he maintains his wrong behavior, he will not come back after the third reincarnation and this soul will be destroyed with no more chance of *Tikun*.

Tikun 'Olam – general Tikun

Evil will disappear from this world and change to goodness, when all the general *Tikunim* - rectifications will be completed[117]. The general *Tikun* is to bring back the world to its former state before the damage caused by the breaking of the vessels. A state of harmony where kindness, bounty and peace prevail and rigors are appeased, when all the fallen sparks of holiness will be bought back up to their origins because of all the positive behavior and acts of men. Consequently, the *Sitra A'hra* (negative force) will not be able to attach and nourish from the higher lights anymore and will cease to exist. G-od gave man an important role in the *Tikun 'Olam* - general *Tikun*. It is now up to him to restore and make the necessary reparations to the world by observing His commandments, doing good deeds, and learning the ways of his Creator.

The final goal is to understand and accomplish His will, to deserve and merit closeness to His presence, and to finally help and participate in the revelation of His unicity to the world.

---

[117] When the fallen sparks will ascend again

Chapter 13

TORAH AND MITSVOT

The Torah contains four levels of comprehension, of which the highest is the Sod (secret). At this level, all the mystical and esoteric knowledge that make up the Kabbalah is revealed. These profound secrets are alluded to in the letters, words and different stories narrated in the Torah. The Torah contains 613 commandments; similarly, there are 613 veins and bones in man, 613 parts to the soul, and 613 lights in each Sephira or Partsuf. This number is not arbitrary, as there are important interrelations and interactions between them.

Torah

The Kabbalah is the mystical and esoteric explanation of the Torah. All the profound secrets explained in the Kabbalah, are alluded to in the letters[118], words and different stories narrated in the Torah. These stories as well as the shape of the letters, the vowels[119], and the cantillation notes are a *Levush* – outer garment on the real message and meaning of the Torah. The different systems of *Sephirot* and configurations of lights and energies are represented by the people[120] and events in the Hebrew texts of the Torah. Therefore, the translations only cover the most basic meaning and can not reach into the real purpose and signification of the Torah as explained in the Zohar:

> "Rabbi Shimon said: Woe to this man who says that the Torah came to simply relate stories in an ordinary language, because if this is so, even in these times we could make a Torah from ordinary tales, and even nicer than from those [tales]. If the Torah came to explain worldly subjects, even the governors of the [present] world have more interesting stories. If so, let's follow what it [tale] says and make a Torah of it in the same way. But really, all that the Torah says is of very high nature, and of supernal secrets.

---

[118] Initials, end letters and more
[119] Each one corresponds to a *Sephira*
[120] The main personalites correspond to *Sephirot* or configurations

153

Therefore, the story in the Torah is the garment of the Torah. The one that thinks that this garment is itself the Torah and that there is nothing else, let his soul swell and have no part in the world to come. For this reason, King David said: (Tehilim, 119. 118) "Open my eyes so I may glaze the wondrous things in your Torah". Meaning what is under this garment of the Torah.

Come and see, there is a garment that is visible to all, the ignorant people that see a man well dressed and which looks distinguished by his clothing, do not look any further and judge him according to his nice garment. They think that the clothing represents the body of man and his body, his soul.

Likewise is the Torah, it has a body which are the commandments called "the body of the Torah". This body is dressed with garments which are the stories of the present world, the ignorant only looks at this garment which is the story in the Torah, not any further, and not at what is under this garment. The ones that know more do not look at the garment but rather at the body under this garment. The wise, the servants of the Lord, the ones that stood at Mount Sinai, only look at the soul of the Torah, which is the essential of all, the real Torah [Kabbalah]. In the future we will look only at the soul of the soul of the Torah.

154

Woe to those sinners that say that the Torah is no more than a story; they are looking at the garment and no more. Praised are the righteous that look in the Torah like it should. Wine is only contained in a jug; similarly the Torah is only contained in this garment, consequently, it is necessary to look solely at what is under this clothing. Therefore, all these matters and stories are only garments."

(*Zohar, Bamidbar, Behalotekha* 58- 64)

The *Torah* has 248 positive and 365 negative commandments. Similarly, there are 613 veins and bones in man, 613 parts to the soul, and 613 lights in each *Sephira* or configuration. This number is not arbitrary, as there are important interrelations and interactions between them.

The Torah contains four levels of comprehension, of which the highest is the *Sod* (secret). At this level, the Torah explains to us the goal of creation, the real purpose of all the commandments and their influence on the *Sephirot*.

Through the knowledge of Kabbalah[121], we can arrive at a level of true understanding of the will of the Creator, His guidance, the creation, and in a way, "decode" the profound secrets of our holy Torah.

---

[121] By understanding the systems of *Sephirot* and configurations, their relationships and illuminations

Mitsvot - commandments

In the Torah there are 613 *Mitsvot* and each one corresponds to one of the 613 veins and bones of man and to one of the 613 parts of his soul. By observing the commandments, man reinforces their strength, and by not accomplishing them, he, in a way, weakens them.

The *Mitsvot* were given for three main reasons:
- To reinforce and purify man
- To act on and influence the guidance
- To help accomplish the *Tikun* of the creation

After the breaking of the vessels and the fall of the 288 sparks, man has to act and participate in the ascent of the fallen sparks to their origin. This can be done by accomplishing the *Mitsvot* and by the prayers. As there are different levels of grasping the meanings and purpose of our actions, there are also various possibilities and powers of influence, depending on the understanding and intention of our acts.

The husks are the manifestations of the negative force to obstruct the lights of the *Sephirot,* and this degradation is caused by the sins committed by man. When accomplishing the *Mitsvot,* the lower beings send positive energies to weaken these husks and detach them from the higher lights, and thus remove any obstacles from the inflows and outflows of positive energies. Therefore, before each prayer and performance of the commandments of the Torah, we try to unify the masculine and feminine configurations so there will be harmony on high, and that a result or inflow of abundance will come down to us.

By understanding the profound meanings of these commandments as explained in the Kabbalah, we realize the enormous love that the Lord bestows to His creatures by allowing them to be part of this dynamic system, and by giving them the means and tools to reach the highest realms.

Chapter 14

GEMATRIA

There are different systems of interpretation of the hidden meanings of the Torah. One of them is the Gematria, where the mathematical values of each letter or word are calculated. Each letter having its own numerical value, the fact that some words have the same total is not just coincidence, but denotes a similarity or complementarity.

Gematria - *Numerical values of the letters*

It is one of the different systems of interpretation of the hidden meanings of the Torah, where mathematical values of letters, words, and sentences are calculated to find a similarity or complementarity. Each letter has its own numerical value.

Letter	Name	Value
א	Aleph	1
ב	Beit	2
ג	Gimel	3
ד	Dalet	4
ה	He	5
ו	Vav	6
ז	Zain	7
ח	'het	8
ט	Tet	9
י	Yud	10
כ	Khaf	20
ל	Lamed	30
מ	Mem	40
נ	Nun	50
ס	Samekh	60
ע	'ain	70
פ	Pey	80
צ	Tsadey	90
ק	Kuf	100
ר	Resh	200
ש	Shin	300
ת	Tav	400

161

The final letters also have their own numerical values:

Letter	Name	Value
ך	Final Khaf	500
ם	Final Mem	600
ן	Final Nun	700
ף	Final Pey	800
ץ	Final Tsadey	900

There are seven main types of *Gematriot*:

- *Ragil* - regular
- *Katan* – small value
- *HaKlali* – value squared
- *Kolel* - regular plus a value for one or all the letters
- *HaKadmi* – regular plus the value of the preceding letters
- *HaPerati* – each letter squared
- *Miluy*- sum of the spellings

1 - *Ragil*: the numbers of the letters are as follows:

From	To	Value
א	ט	1 - 9
י	צ	10 -90
ק	ת	100 - 400
ך	ץ	500 -900

Ex : הארץ = 1106

2 – *Katan*: tens and hundreds are reduced to one digit.

From	To	Value
א	ט	1 - 9
י	צ	1 - 9
ק	ת	1 - 4
ך	ץ	5 -9

Ex : הארץ = 17

3 – *HaKlali*: the *Ragil* value of the word squared.

Ex : הארץ = 1106 * 1106 = 1 223 236

4 – *Kolel*: the *Ragil* value of the word + the numbers of letters, or + 1 for the word.

Ex : הארץ = 1106 + 4 = 1110
       or 1106 + 1 = 1107

5 – *HaKadmi*: each letter has its *Ragil* value plus the total of all the ones preceding it.

From	To	Value
א	ט	1 - 45
י	צ	55 – 495
ק	ת	595 –1495
ך	ץ	1995 – 4995

Ex : הארץ = 15+1+795+4995 = 5806

6 – *HaPerati*: each letter is squared.

Ex : הארץ = 5 * 5 = 25, 1 * 1 = 1
200 * 200 = 40 000, 900 * 900 = 810 000 Total = 850 026

7 – *Miluy:* the sum of the spelling of each letter.

Letter	Miluy	Value
ה	הא	6
א	אלף	111
ר	ריש	510
ץ	צדי	104

Ex : הארץ = 731

By the *Gematriot*, we see that each letter and word has a dynamic meaning beyond the simple definitions. Gematria is only one of the secret ways of interpreting the hidden meanings in the Torah.

There are also permutation systems where letters are replaced by others in a set order as "ATBaSH" where the first letter is replaced by the last, the second by the one before the last etc. "Notrikun", where initials of different words make a new word, and many other systems.

Chapter 15

HISTORY OF THE KABBALAH

The History of the Kabbalah can be traced back to Avraham the patriarch who wrote the "Sepher HaYetsira"- Book of formation. Since then, many developments following the wandering of the Jewish people in the different continents, further clarified its concepts.

First period – The beginning
Aprox. 1750 B.C.E, Israel

Tradition has it that one of the first writings of the Kabbalah, called *"Sepher HaYetsira"* (The Book of Formation), was composed by Avraham Avinu. It is the first book that mentions a system of ten lights called *Sephirot.*

Second period – The Zohar
Aprox. 240 C.E, Israel

Rabbi Shim'on Bar Yo'hay lived in Galilee in the second century and was a disciple of Rabbi 'Akiva. To escape the Romans, he went into hiding with his son Rabbi El'azar into a cave for thirteen years. During this time, he composed the Zohar, which is the esoteric and mystical explanation of the Torah, and the base of most of the Kabbalah writings.

Third Period – Printing of the Zohar
1270, Spain

After having disappeared for about one thousand years, the book of the Zohar is found and printed by Rabbi Moshe de Leon in Spain. This new printing will be disseminated all over Europe, North Africa and the Middle-East and will allow a wider learning of its writings. It is also the period of the "Prophetic Kabbalah" as taught by Rabbi Abraham Abul'afia.

167

The three Kabbalah schools in Europe
1200 - 1300

In the cities of Provence in France, Gerona in Spain, and Worms in Germany were formed three of the main centers of Kabbalah of that period. Under prominent Kabbalists as Rabbi Its'hak the Blind, Rabbi Ezra of Gerona, Rabbi El'azar of Worms, Na'hmanide and others, essential works were published as *"Sepher HaBahir" "Sepher Ha'Hesed"* and important commentaries on *"Sepher HaYetsira"*.

In France, a type of contemplative mysticism was developed with meditation on the prayers and *Sephirot*. In Spain, an effort was made to bring the major ideas of the Kabbalah to a wider public. In Germany, Rabbi El'azar of Worms had declared that G-od is even closer to the universe and man, than the soul is to the body.

The Tsfat Kabbalists
1500, Tsfat, Israel

After the expulsion from Spain in 1492, some important Spanish Kabbalists as Rabbi Moshe Kordovero, Rabbi Shlomo Alkabetz and Rabbi Yoseph Karo moved to the city of Tsfat in Israel. There, a school of Kabbalah was founded named "New Kabbalah" or "Kabbalah of Tsfat". It is the golden era of the Kabbalah. After this first generation, Rabbi Its'hak Luria Ashkenazi, the Ari Z'al, who was born in Jerusalem, became the leading Kabbalist in Tsfat. He explained and clarified all the main concepts of the Kabbalah, and also innovated in the explanation of the *Sephirot* and *Partsufim (configurations)*. He is the author of the corpus *"'Ets 'Haim"*, which contains all his works in the style of *Sha'are* (entrances), and is today the major reference in Kabbalah.

Shabbetai Tsevi
1626-1676

During the 16th century with the coming of Shabbetai Tsevi, who was called the "Kabbalistic Messiah", the Jewish community was divided between his followers and the non-believers. After converting to Islam, this false Messiah caused a big deception and mistrust of the teachings of the Kabbalah. The rabbinical authorities of the time became even more severe toward the learning of Kabbalah, and some were persecuted for learning or writing on the subject.

'Hassidic movement
1700, Eastern Europe

The *'Hassidic* period began with the Ba'al Shem Tov, the founder of the *'Hassidic* movement. He declared the whole universe, mind, and matter to be a manifestation of G-od, and that whoever maintains that this life is worthless is in error. It is worth a great deal; only one must know how to use it properly. The Ba'al Shem Tov's teachings were largely based upon the Kabalistic teachings of the Ari Z'al, but his approach made the benefits of these teachings accessible even to the simplest Jew. Some of the other important leaders that founded their own *'Hassidic* movement are Rabbi Na'hman of Breslev, great grandson of the Baal Shem Tov, and Rabbi Shneur Zalman of Liadi, the *"Ba'al HaTanya"*, founder of the 'Habad Lubavitch movement.

European masters

1700, Europe

At the same time, there were other important authorities of the Kabbalah in other parts of Europe such as Rabbi Moshe 'Haim Luzzatto – Ram'hal - who lived in Italy and Amsterdam. From an early age, the Ram'hal had shown an exceptional talent for the study of Kabbalah; it is said that when he was only fourteen, he already knew all the Kabbalah of the Ari Z'al by heart, and nobody knew about it, not even his parents. He was a very prolific writer and wrote on all aspects of the Torah and the Kabbalah; however, because of false accusations, he sadly was persecuted for most of his short life.

Rabbi Eliyahu of Vilna - The Gaon of Vilna who was born in Lithuania was one of the main leaders of the *Mitnagdim* (opponents to the *'Hasidic* movement). He is considered to be one of the greatest Torah scholar and Kabbalist of the past two centuries.

Sephardic masters
1700 – North and Middle Africa

On the other continent the study of the Kabbalah and mostly the Zohar was also widely spread. Some important scholars are Rabbi Shalom Shar'abi - The Rashash who came from Yemen. He is known as the "Master of the *Kavanot*". Rabbi Ya'acov Abe'htsera, born in Morocco, composed works on all facets of the Torah, including important commentaries on the Kabbalistic explanations of the Torah. Also from Morocco was Rabbi 'Haim Ben 'Atar – Or Ha'Haim. The Ba'al Shem Tov was convinced that the Or Ha'Haim was the Moshia'h of that generation. His main work is the commentary on the Torah; "Or Ha'Haim". Rabbi Yosef 'Haim – The Ben Ish 'Hai, was born in Iraq. He explained the *Halakhot* (laws) on the Kabbalistic level but in an accessible language.

The latest Kabbalists
1900 - Israel

Since the beginning of this century, Israel is considered to be the main centre of Kabbalah. One of the most important contemporary Kabbalists was Rabbi Yehudah Ashlag who was born in Poland in 1886, and died in Israel in 1955. His main work is the translation of all the Zohar from Aramaic to Hebrew, called *"HaSulam"*. Other important Kabbalists are Rabbi Israel Abe'htsera - Baba Sali (1890-1984), Rabbi Yehudah Tzvi Brandwein (1904-1969), Rabbi Avraham Yitzchak HaCohen Kook (1865-1935), Rabbi Yehudah Fatiyah (1859-1942) and others.

171

Each one of these great Kabbalah scholars brought his own explanations and innovations to this marvelous science. Altogether, they left a wealth of writings on the Kabbalah that we hope will one day be more available to the serious learner and seeker of the true Kabbalah.

Chapter 16

KABBALISTS

Since the publication of the Zohar by Rabbi Shim'on Bar Yo'hay, various authors made a difference by further explaining and developing the concepts of Kabbalah.

Rabbi Shim'on Bar Yo'hay

Born in Galilee and died in Meron, Israel during the 2nd century.

Rabbi Shim'on Bar Yo'hay was a disciple of *Rabbi Akiva*. To escape the Romans, he went into hiding with his son *Rabbi El'azar* into a cave for thirteen years. During this time, he composed the *Zohar*, which is the esoteric and mystical explanation of the Torah, and the base for most of the Kabbalah writings.

Rabbi Moshe Ben Na'hman (Na'hmanides) - Ramban

Born in Gerona in 1195, died in Israel 1270

Like Rambam before him, Na'hmanides was both a physician and a great Torah scholar. However, unlike the Rambam, he was also knowledgeable in the Zohar and Kabbalah and wrote a mystical commentary on the Torah. The Ari Z'al had confirmed the depth and reliability of the mystical portion of Ramban's Torah commentary

Na'hmanides also declared that it is a *Mitsva* to live in Israel. He moved and lived there until the end of his life.

175

Rabbi Moshe de Leon

Born in Spain 1240 - 1305

Rabbi Moshe de Leon published the manuscripts of the Zohar that had come into his possession. Some accredited him with its authorship as well, but none of the main Kabbalists agree with that.

Rabbi Abraham Abul'afia

Born in Saragossa in 1240, died in Greece after 1291.

Rabbi Abraham Abul'afia is the precursor of what is called the "Prophetical Kabbalah" where combinations and permutations of *Autiot* (letters), numerals and *Nikud* (vowels) are symbols that explain and disclose the deepest esoteric meanings. Some of his best known works are "*Sefer ha-Ot*" and "*Imre Shefer*".

Rabbi Yosef Gikatila

Born Castille in 1248 - 1310

Between 1272 and 1274, Rabbi Yosef Gikatila studied with Rabbi Abraham Abul'afia, who praised him as his most successful student. He wrote "*Ginat Egoz*", "*Shaarei Orah*", "*Shaarei Tzedek*", and "*Shaar HaNikud*". He was apparently friendly with Moshe de Leon.

Rabbi Moshe Kordovero

Born in 1522, died in Tsfat in 1570.

Rabbi Moshe Kordovero was the founder of the Kabbalah academy in Tsfat. One of his best known student was Rabbi 'Haim Vital. He foresaw the coming of the teachings of the Ari Z'al and admitted in advance their truthfulness. Some of his main works are *"Tomer Deborah"*,*"Pardes Rimonim"*, and *"Or Yakar"*.

Ari Z'al - Rabbi Its'hak Luria Ashkenazi

Born in Jerusalem in 1534, died in 1572 in Tsfat.

The Ari Z'al, Rabbi Its'hak Luria Ashkenazi was the leading Kabbalist in Tsfat; he explained and clarified all the main concepts of the Kabbalah. He also made innovations in the explanation of the *Sephirot* and *Partsufim* (configurations). He is the author of the corpus *"Kitve HaAri"*, which contains all his works in the style of *Sha'are* (entrances). His main works are the *"Ets 'Haim"*, *"Sha'ar Hagilgulim"*, *"Sha'ar Hakavanot"*.

Rabbi Meir Poppers

Died in Israel in 1622.

Rabbi Meir Poppers was one of the important Kabbalists in the circle of the Ari Z'al. He is best known for putting in order Rabbi 'Haim Vital's manuscripts of the teachings of the Ari Z'al and printing them. Rabbi Meir himself wrote several important Kabbalistic works.

Rabbi Shmuel Vital

Born in Damascus, died in Egypt in the 17th century

Rabbi Shmuel Vital was the son of Rabbi 'Haim Vital. He had inherited many of his father's manuscripts of the Kabbalistic teachings of the Ari Z'al. He arranged these into eight categories, known as the Shmoneh She'arim (eight gates). He also wrote several Kabbalistic works of his own.

Ba'al Shem Tov
Rabbi Israel Ben Eliezer

Born in 1698 in Russia, died in Ukraine in 1760

Ba'al Shem Tov was the founder of the *'Hassidic* movement. He declared the whole universe, mind, and matter to be a manifestation of G-od, and that whoever maintains that this life is worthless is in error. It is worth a great deal; only one must know how to use it properly. A living legend, the *Ba'al Shem Tov* spent most of his time in worship, serving G-od, teaching his disciples, and giving blessings to the thousands that came to see him.

One of his favorite sayings was that no man has sunk too low to be able to raise himself to G-od.

Rabbi Moshe 'Haim Luzzatto – Ram'hal

Born in Padua, Italy in 1707, died in Israel in 1746.

Rabbi Moshe 'Haim Luzzatto showed at an early age an exceptional talent for the study of Kabbalah. It is said that when he was only fourteen, he already knew all the Kabbalah of the Ari Z'al by heart, and nobody knew about it, not even his parents. He was a very prolific writer and wrote on all aspects of the Torah and the Kabbalah. Some of his main works are *"Kala'h Pit'he 'Hokhma"* ,*"Klalut Hailan"*, and *"Adir Bamaron"*.

Rabbi Eliyahu of Vilna - The Gaon of Vilna

Born in Vilna, Lithuania, died in Vilna in 1797.

Rabbi Eliyahu of Vilna was one of the main leaders of the *Mitnagdim* (opponents to the *'Hasidic* movement). He is considered to be one of the greatest Torah scholars and

179

Kabbalists of the past two centuries. Among his works on the Kabbalah are *"Kitvei HaGra Be'eniene Kabbalah"*

Rabbi Shalom Shar'abi - The Rashash

Born in Shar'ab, Yemen in 1720, died in Jerusalem in 1777.

After leaving Yemen, Rabbi Shalom Shar'abi joined the *Yeshiva* of the *Mekubalim "Beth El"* in Jerusalem. He is known as the "Master of the *Kavanot"*. His *"Siddur HaRashash"* is the *Siddur* (prayer book) used by some Kabbalists in their everyday prayers, and is based on the *Kavanot* of the Ari Z'al.

Rabbi Shneur Zalman of Liadi – The Alter Rebbe

Born in Russia, 1745, died in Russia in 1813.

Rabbi S. Zalman of Liadi is also called *"Baal HaTanya"*, he is the founder of the 'Habad - Lubavitch movement and was a descendant of the *Maharal of Prague*. He studied under the *Maggid of Mezritch* the writings of the Ari, and composed the *"Tanya"*.

Rabbi Na'hman of Breslev

Born in Russia in 1772, died in Uman, Russia in 1811

Rabbi Na'hman was the great grandson of the Ba'al Shem Tov. He gave great importance to *"Dvekut"* (attachment to G-od) and pure joy. Some of his main works are *"Likutey Moharan"*, *"Tikun HaKlali"*, and his well known stories and fables.

Rabbi Ya'acov Abe'htsera

Born in Morocco in 1808, died in Dimanhur, Egypt, 1880.

Rabbi Ya'acov was a Kabbalist renowned for his piety and for performing miracles. He composed works on all facets of the Torah, including important commentaries on the Kabbalistic explanation of the Torah. Some of his main works are *"Makhsof HaLavan"* and *"Pitu'he 'Hotam"*.

Rabbi Yosef 'Haim – Ben Ish 'Hai,

Born and died in Iraq 1834 – 1909

Ben Ish 'Hai was a prolific author who wrote at incredible speed. It is known that he would finish writing a complete page before the ink at the top of the page had dried. He explained the *Halakhot* (laws) on the Kabbalistic level but in an accessible language.

181

Rabbi Yehudah Ashlag

Born in Poland 1886, died in Israel in 1955.

Rabbi Yehudah Ashlag was one of the main contemporary Kabbalists. His main work is the translation of all the Zohar from Aramaic to Hebrew called "*HaSulam*" and "*Talmud 'Eser HaSephirot*".

Transliteration of the letters

Letter	Name	Equivalent	Transliteration
א	Aleph	A, O, E, I	A, O, E, I
ב	Beit	B, V	B, V
ג	Gimel	G	G
ד	Dalet	D	D
ה	He	H	H
ו	Vav	V	V
ז	Zain	Z	Z
ח	'het		'h
ט	Tet	T	T
י	Yud	Y	Y
כ	Khaf	C, K, KH	C, K, KH
ל	Lamed	L	L
מ	Mem	M	M
נ	Nun	N	N
ס	Samekh	S	S
ע	'ain		'
פ	Pey	P, F	P, F
צ	Tsadey	TS	TS
ק	Kuf	C, K	C, K
ר	Resh	R	R
ש	Shin	S, SH	S, SH
ת	Tav	T	T

GLOSSARY

א"ק
A"K
Adam Kadmon - *Initials*

אבא
Abah
Partsuf Abah – Father
One of the five main configurations. It is the *Sephira 'Hokhma*.

אבא ואמא
Abah ve Imah
Partsufim Abah and Imah
These two *Partsufim (configurations)* are essential for the guidance of the worlds, *Abah* is the *Sephira 'Hokhma, Imah* is the *Sephira Binah*.

אבחנה
Av'hana
Distinction – Insight
Understanding of the deeper meaning or Kabbalistic interpretation.

אבר
Ever
Organ – Limb (Anthropomorphism)
In the language of Kabbalah, anthropomorphisms are used only to illustrate the esoteric power of these forces. It is, of course, understood that they are no physical representations of what resides in the higher realms.

187

אדם קדמון
Adam Kadmon
Primordial man - World above Atsilut
This is the first configuration, or the first world where the emanated lights were formed into ten straight *Sephirot.*

אדנ- י
Adona-y
One of the names of G-od, represented by the *Sephira Malkhut.* It is also the feminine representation of His presence.

אהי-ה
AHY-H
One of the names of G-od, represented by the *Sephira Keter.*

אור
Or
Light
The term used to describe an emanation, a force or energy.

אחור
A'hor
Backside – Behind
In general, it represents rigor.

אחר
A'her
Other

Name also used for the other side or negative force.

אילן

Ilan

Tree

The disposition of the *Sephirot* into the three-pillar arrangement is called the *Sephirotic* tree.

אין סוף

Ein Sof

The without end or limit – Infinite

One of the names of G-od.

The Name of G-od that is the most used in the Kabbalah.

אלוה-ים

Elohi-m

One of the names of G-od, represented by the *Sephira Gevurah*. In general, it denotes rigor in the actions of G-od.

אמא

Imah

Partsuf Imah - Mother

One of the five main configurations. It is the *Sephira Binah*.

אצילות

Atsilut

World of Emanation

It is the highest of the four worlds, above the worlds of *Beriah*, *Yetsirah* and *'Asiah*. From *Atsilut* unfolded all the lower worlds, which are the source of existence for the physical worlds.

אצילות בריאה יצירה עשייה
Atsilut, Beriah, Yetsirah and 'Asiah

From the first configuration, *Adam Kadmon* (*Primordial man*), emanations made the four lower worlds.

The first world is *Atsilut* – the world of emanation. Under the partition of *Atsilut* is the world of *Beriah* (creation) - the world of the *Neshamot* (souls). Under the partition of *Beriah* is the world of *Yetsirah* (formation) - the world of the angels. Under the partition of *Yetsirah* is the world of *'Asiah* (action) - the physical world.

ארי ז"ל
Ari Z'al
Rabbi Its'hak Luria Ashkenazi

Born in Jerusalem in 1534, died in 1572 in Tsfat, Israel.
He was the leading Kabbalist in Tsfat. He explained and clarified all the main concepts of the Kabbalah. He is the author of the *"Ets 'Haim"*.

אריך אנפין
Arikh Anpin
Partsuf – Long countenance

It is the main *Partsuf* (configuration) in each world. All the other *Partsufim* are his "branches".

אתב"ש
ATBaSH

Permutation of letters to understand hidden meanings of words. First letter replaced by the last, second by the one before the last etc.

190

ב"ן
BaN (52)
Miluy (spelling) of the name ה-ו-ה-י **with a total of 52**
It corresponds to the feminine aspect - rigor.

בינה
Binah
Sephira (understanding)
Third of the *Sephirot*.

ברוך הוא
Barukh Hu, or B'H
Blessed He is
Used after the pronunciation or writing of G-od's names.

בריאה
Beriah
World of creation – of the souls
The second world to unfold is called *Beriah*; the world of creation. It is the world of the *Neshamot* (souls). It is under *Atsilut* and above *Yetsirah* and *'Asiah*.

בר יוחאי
Bar Yo'hay
Rabbi Shim'on Bar Yo'hay
To escape the Romans, he went into hiding with his son Rabbi El'azar into a cave for thirteen years and composed the Zohar.

ברכה

Berakhah

Blessing

When saying the blessing with the Kabbalistic meditation on the appropriate words or names, we act and participate directly on the *Tikun* (repair) of the thing being blessed.

ג' ראשונות

Shalosh Rishonot

The three first Sephirot

Keter, 'Hokhma, Binah

ג"ר

G"aR

The three first Sephirot

Keter, 'Hokhma, Binah

גבול

Gevul

Boundary – Limit

By placing boundaries upon His light, the Creator revealed the concepts of rigor and limit needed by the created beings, and gave a space for all the created to exist.

גבורה

Gevurah

Rigor

The outcome of His light, once filtered by the *Sephira Gevurah,* emanates rigor. Rigor is mostly manifested by all the feminine aspects as the name of *BaN (52),* the *Sephira Gevurah,* and by all the concealments of the masculine

192

aspects that represent bounty.

גבורה
Gevurah
Sephira (Rigor)
Fifth of the *Sephirot*.

גימטריה
Gematria
Numerical values of the letters
Each letter has its own numerical value. The fact that some words have the same numerical value is not just coincidence, but denotes a similarity or complementarity.

גלגול
Gilgul
Reincarnation
The *Tikun* of the soul is realized by the *Gilgul* (reincarnation), and by the *'Ibur* (attachment). The *Gilgul* is the reincarnation of a soul from the time of birth until death.

גן עדן
Gan 'Eden
The Garden of Eden
The place of rest for the *Neshamot* (souls) after their separation from their former physical bodies. There is a lower and a higher *Gan 'Eden*.

גן עדן עליון
Gan 'Eden 'Elyon
The upper Garden of Eden

In the higher *Gan 'Eden*, the *Neshamot* (souls) are enjoying pure spiritual pleasures, and do not have any spiritual image resembling their former bodies.

גן עדן תחתון
Gan' Eden Takhton
The lower Garden of Eden
In the lower *Gan 'Eden*, the *Neshamot* (souls) are enjoying spiritual pleasures but still have a spiritual body resembling their former bodies.

גשמיות
Gashmiut
Corporeality
Potential existence for separated entities became possible only once distanced from the intensity of His light. The greater the distance the more corporality is possible.

דו"ן
D"uN
Masculine and feminine
Initials

דוכרין ונוקבין
Dukhrin Ve Nukvin
Masculine and feminine
See Mayin Dukhrin, Mayin Nukvin

דומם, צומח, חי, מדבר
Domem, Tsomeakh, 'Hay, Medaber
Mineral, vegetal, animal and the speaking

194

Parallel to the four worlds of *Atsilut, Beriah, Yetsirah* and *'Asiah,* there are four types of existence in our world: mineral, vegetal, animal and the speaking.

דעת
Da'at
Sephira (Knowledge)
Fourth of the *Sephirot.*

דעת
Da'at
Knowledge
The essential knowledge is the one of the will of the Creator and His ways of guidance in this existence, as explained in the Kabbalah.

הארה
Hearah
Illumination
Special outburst of a light for a specific purpose.

הוד
Hod
Sephira – Glory
Eighth of the *Sephirot.*

הוי"ה
HaVaYaH
One of the ways of mentioning the Tetragamon
יְ-ה-ו-ה without pronouncing it.

היכל

Hekhal

Portal – Level

The *Hekhalot* are the different levels of ascension of the prayers before reaching the *'Olam Atsilut* during the *Amidah*.

הנהגה

Hanhagah

Guidance

The guidance of the worlds is done through the influence of the different *Sephirot* and *Partsufim (configurations)*.

הרחקה

Har'hakah

Distancing

Distance denotes a contrary or a non compatibility.

Potential for existence for separated entities became possible only once distanced from the intensity of His light.

השגה

Hasagah

Attainment – Comprehension

To reach a higher level of understanding or comprehension, one has to make the effort of studying the *Sod* (secret) of the Torah, which is the Kabbalah.

השתלשלות

Hishtalshelut

Evolution - Chain of events

In the Kabbalah, the *Hishtalshelut* is the chain of events starting from the first act of G-od in this creation, which is the

196

"*Tsimtsum*" *(retraction)*, until the complex arrangements that make the guidance of the worlds.

ז' מלכים
Sheva' Malkhin
Seven kings
The seven kings of Edom that died (Bereshit, 36, 31) correspond to the seven lower *Sephirot* that broke during the *Shvirat HaKelim* (breaking of the vessels).

ז"א
Z'A
Zeir Anpin (Small countenance)
Initials of configuration *Zeir Anpin*, used more often than the full name.
See Zeir Anpin

ז"ת
Za"T
Zain Takhtonot
Seven lower *Sephirot*

זו"ן
Z"UN
Zeir Anpin and Nukva
Initials of configuration *Zeir Anpin and Nukva*, used more often than the full names.

זוהר
Zohar
The book of splendor, written by Rabbi Shim'on Bar Yo'hay.

The *Zohar* is the esoteric and mystical explanation of the Torah, and the base for most of the Kabbalah writings.

זיו
Ziv
Radiance – Illumination
A superior light will radiate to a lower one to influence it, or to create a new emanation.

זיווג
Zivug
Union
The *Zivug* is the union of the masculine with its feminine. All the outcomes of the higher emanations are a result of the different unions of the masculine and feminine lights.

זין תחתונות
Zayin Takhtonot
Seven lower
The seven lower *Sephirot*:
'*Hesed*, *Gevurah*, *Tiferet*, *Netsa'h*, *Hod*, *Yesod*, and *Malkhut*.

זכר
Zakhar
Masculine
There are masculine *Partsufim* that bestow kindness, and feminine *Partsufim* that bestow rigor. By their union, different equilibriums of these two forces (kindness and rigor), make the guidance.

זעיר אנפין

Zeir Anpin

Partsuf Zeir Anpin - Small countenance

Configuration *Zeir Anpin (Z'A)* is composed of the six lower *Sephirot: 'Hesed, Gevurah, Tiferet, Netsa'h, Hod, Yesod.*

חבד

'HaBaD

'Hokhma, Binah and Da'at

Initials of the first triplet of the *Sephirot: 'Hokhma, Binah and Da'at.*

חגת

'HaGaT

'Hesed, Gevurah and Tiferet

Initials of the second triplet of the *Sephirot: 'Hesed, Gevurah, and Tiferet.*

חומר

'Homer

Material – Physical

Materiality is only found in the lower world of *'Asiah* – action.

חוץ

'Huts

Outside

Denotes a position of non-compatibility or a contrary.

חושך

'Hoshekh

Darkness

State of distance from the *Kedushah* and closeness to the *Sitra A'hra* (negative side).

חיבור
'Hibur
Attachment
All the *Sephirot* and *Partsufim* have a certain degree of attachment between them.

חיה
'Haya
Fourth level of the soul
'Haya is the fourth level and can only be acquired after the preceding levels.

חיות
'Hayut
Livelihood
The livelihood of everything, whether positive or negative, has only one origin; G-od the Creator and sustainer of all.

חיצוניות
'Hitsoniut
Exteriority (The)
The external or negative force – *Sitra A'hra* is also called exteriority.

חכמה
'Hokhma
Sephira – Wisdom
Second of the *Sephirot*.

חכמת האמת
'Hokhmat HaEmet
Knowledge of the truth
One of the names of the Kabbalah.

חלל
'Hallal
Space – Vacuum
The space left by the *Tsimtsum* (retraction) of His light.

חסד
'Hesed
Bounty – Kindness
Kindness is manifested by the different positioning and interactions of the masculine and feminine *Partsufim*.

חסד
'Hesed
Sephira (Bounty)
Fourth of the *Sephirot*.

חסד, גבורה, תפארת
'Hesed, Gevurah and Tiferet
Second triplet of the *Sephirot*.

טמא
Tameh
Impure
State of distance from the *Kedushah* and closeness to the *Sitra A'hra* (negative force).

י-ה ו ה

Adona-y

Y-H-V-H *Tetragamon* (י-ה-ו-ה)

Main name of G-od, reveals kindness and mercy, represented by the *Sephira Tiferet*. The creative forces or energies are the different powers in the letters of the name of G-od י-ה-ו-ה, and the various letters added to make their different spellings.

יום

Yom

Day

Each new day is of a new emanation that governs it.

יחוד

Yi'hud

Unification – Union

The union of the *Sephirot* or *Partsufim* for the *Zivug* and for the descent of the abundance.

יחודו

Yi'hudo

His unicity

The light of G-od is unique, of equal force, quality and beyond all description.

יחידה

Ye'hida

Fifth level of the soul

Ye'hida is the fifth level and can only be acquired after the preceding levels.

יסוד
Yesod
Sephira (Foundation)
Ninth of the *Sephirot*.

יצירה
Yetsirah
World of formation – of the angels
The third world to unfold is called *Yetsirah*, the world of formation, the world of the angels. It is under *Atsilut* and *Beriah* and above *'Asiah*.

יצר
Yetser
Instinct – Impulse
The *Yetser Hatov* corresponds to the good or positive impulse in man, The *Yetser Hara'* is his bad or negative impulse.

ירושלים
Yerushalaim
Jerusalem
The closest place to G-od's emanations.

ישסו"ת
ISOT
Partsufim Israel Saba and Tevunah
Initials

ישסו"ת ב
ISOT 2
Second Partsufim of Israel Saba and Tevunah

Initials

כוונה
Kavanah
Intention – Concentration
A first level of praying with *Kavanah* is to understand the words and to concentrate, A second level is to know and concentrate on the permutation and the different names of G-od, their purpose and goal in this particular prayer.

כחב
Ka'HaB
Keter, 'Hokhma, Binah
Initials

כיסא
Kisey
Throne
There are three main types of thrones:
Kisey HaDin - throne of justice
Kisey Hakavod - throne of glory
Kisey Ra'hamim - throne of mercy

כלי
Keli
Recipient –Vessel
Each *Sephira* is composed of a vessel called *Keli*, which holds its part of light called *Or.*

כתר

Keter

Sephira – Crown

First and most important of the *Sephirot*.

כתר, חכמה, בינה

Keter, 'Hokhma, Binah

The three first *Sephirot*, often referred as the *Ga'R*; *Shalosh Rishonot* (the three first ones).

לאה

Leah

Leah - Partsuf Nukva

The configuration *Nukva* comprises two distinct *Partsufim* (configurations): *Ra'hel* and *Leah*. Configuration *Leah* is of the aspect of rigor.

להחמיר

LeHa'hmir

To be more stringent

A strict observance of all the details when accomplishing a *Mitsva* or *Tefilah*.

לוצאטו

Luzzatto

Rabbi Moshe 'Haim Luzzatto – Ram'hal

Born in Padua, Italy in 1707, died in Israel in 1746.

Rabbi Moshe 'Haim Luzzatto was a very prolific writer and wrote on the all aspects of the Torah and the Kabbalah.

לקבל

Lekabel

To receive

The word Kabbalah comes from the verb *Lekabel* (to receive); however, in order to receive it is first necessary to want, and to become a *Keli* (recipient) able to receive and contain this knowledge.

מ"ה

MaH (45)

Miluy (spelling) of the name י-ה-ו-ה with a total of 45

The name of *MaH (45)* is the *Miluyim* (spelling) of א, which is a (ו) (Vav) line in the middle (mercy) that unites two י (Yud) (kindness and rigor). It is of a masculine aspect and represents mercy.

מ"ן

M"N

Mayin Nukvin (feminine waters)

Initials

מוחין

Mo'hin

Brains

The *Mo'hin* are the directive force given to the *Partsuf* (configuration).

מיין דוכרין

Mayin Dukhrin

Masculine waters

One of two emanations allegorically called masculine waters.

מיין נוקבין

Mayin Nukvin

Feminine waters

One of two emanations allegorically called feminine waters.

מילוי

Miluy

Spelling

Depending on which letters are used, the numerical value of a name changes, and each one of these possibilities becomes different in its nature and actions.

מלאכים

Malakhim

Angels

The world of the angels is the third world - *'Olam Yetsirah* - the world of formation.

מלכות

Malkhut

Sephira (Royalty)

Tenth of the *Sephirot*.

מעשה בראשית

Ma'ase Bereshit

Works or acts of the creation

Name given for all the details of the beginning of creation, from the *Tsimtsum*, the first worlds, the *Sephirot* etc.

מעשה המרקבה

Ma'ase Hamerkava

Works or acts of the Heavenly Chariot

Name given for all the details of the *Sephirot, Partsufim, Tikunim* and *Zivugim* that make the guidance.

מצוה

Mitsva

Commandment

The *Torah* has 248 positive and 365 negative commandments. Similarly, there are 613 veins and bones in man, 613 parts to the soul, and 613 lights in each *Sephira* or configuration. Each one of the 613 *Mitsvot* corresponds to one of the 613 veins and bones of man and to one of the 613 parts of his soul.

מקובל

Mekubal

Kabbalist - Accepted

A *Mekubal* is a person who is accepted to receive this knowledge, and is able to hold it by living in the path of Torah and rightness to strengthen himself constantly.

מקום

Makom

Place – space

Until the world was created, He and His Name were One. He willed to create, and thus contracted His light to create all beings by giving them a space.

מקור

Makor

Source – Origin

Each emanation has its source in the higher realms

מרקבה
Merkavah
Heavenly chariot
The *Partsufim* (configurations), *Sephirot* and the *Sephirotic* tree, with all their inter-relations, actions, and illuminations.

משל
Mashal
Allegory
Sometimes used to explain or illustrate difficult concepts.

מתלבש
Mitlabesh
Dress
Partsufim dress on, or in, each other. The more important *Partsuf* will dress inside the less important to direct him.

נהי
NeHY
Netsa'h, Hod and Yesod
Initials of the third triplet of the *Sephirot: Netsa'h, Hod and Yesod.*

נוטריקון
Notrikun (acronym)
Notrikun is a method of interpretation in which the initials of different words make a new word.
אל מלך נאמן = אמן

נוקבא

Nukva

Feminine - Sephira Malkhut – configurations Ra'hel, Leah

The configuration *Nukva* represents the feminine – the principle of receiving. It comprises two distinct configurations : *Ra'hel* and *Leah.*

ניצוצות

Nitsutsot

Sparks

To sustain the *Kelim* after they broke, 288 sparks of their lights came down as well, because a connection to their original lights was needed to keep them alive.

נמשל

Nimshal

Moral

Sometimes used to explain or illustrate difficult concepts.

נפש

Nefesh

Soul - First level of the soul

Nefesh is the first and lower level of the soul.

נפש, רוח, נשמה, חיה, יחידה

Nefesh, Rua'h, Neshama, 'Haya and Ye'hida

The soul has five names: *Nefesh, Rua'h, Neshama, 'Haya* and *Ye'hida*, which correspond to its five levels.

נצח

Netsa'h

Sephira (splendor)

Seventh of the *Sephirot*.

נקבה

Nekevah

Female – Feminine

Rigor is manifested by all the feminine aspects and by the concealment of the masculine aspects, which represent bounty.

נקודות

Nekudot

Punctuation – Vowels – Points

Each vowel corresponds to a *Sephira.* In a way, It translates, with the combination of the letters, the inner identity of the word.

נר"ן

NaRaN

Nefesh, Rua'h, Neshama

Initials of the first three levels of the soul.

נשמה

Neshama

Soul - Third level of the soul

Neshama is the third level and can be acquired only after acquiring the levels of *Nefesh* and *Rua'h.*

ס"ג

SaG (63)

Miluy (spelling) of the name י-ה-ו-ה with a total of 63

The name of *SaG* is the second level of the four names for a total of 63.

ס"מ

S"M

initials of the main destructive Angel

סגולה

Segulah

Remedy – Protection

Names or combinations of names of angels with special signs or incantations, written on parchment to protect, or to invoke particular powers.

סוד - סודות

Sod - ot

Secret –s

Through the knowledge of Kabbalah, we can reach a level of true understanding, and in a way "decode" the profound secrets of the Torah.

סיטרא אחרא

Sitra A'hra

Negative force

The root of the *Sitra A'hra* is in the lack or absence of the *Kedushah*.

ספירה
Sephira
The light of G-od is unique and of equal force and quality. In a way, a *Sephira* is a "filter" that transforms this light into a particular force or attribute, by which the Creator guides the worlds.

ספירות
Sephirot
Plural of Sephira
See Sephira

ספירות הישר
Sephirot HaYashar
Straight Sephirot
Sephirot arranged in three columns: right, left and middle, representing the guidance of the world in the manner of Kindness, rigor and mercy.

ספירות העיגולים
Sephirot Ha'Igulim
Encircling Sephirot
These ten *Sephirot* are in charge of the general guidance of the worlds and are not influenced by the actions of men.

ע"ב
'A"V
Miluy (spelling) of the name י-ה-ו-ה with a total of 72
The name *'A"V* is the highest level of the four names of *'A"V*, *SaG, MaH (45)* and *BaN (52)*.

213

עב, סג מה, בן
'A"V, SaG, MaH, BaN

Spellings of the Name י-ה-ו-ה

'A"V (72), SaG (63), MaH (45), BaN (52)

The creative forces or energies are the different powers in the four letters of the name of G-od י-ה-ו-ה, and the various letters added to make their different spellings.

עבודה
'Avodah

Service – Duty

One of the main goals of all the works, deeds and prayers of men in this existence is to help and participate in the ascent of the fallen 288 sparks to their origin.

עולם
'Olam

World

A *'Olam* is a possibility and a type of existence in a particular dimension.

עשיה
'Asiah

World of action – of man

The fourth world to unfold is called *'Asiah* - action, the world of physical existence.

עשר
'Eser

Ten

Number of *Sephirot* in each world, *Sephira, Partsuf* or

configuration.

עת

'Et

Time – Moment

Each moment can be described in terms of a permutation of the names of G-od, and by the various *Sephirot and Partsufim.*

עתיק יומין

'Atik Yomin

Partsuf – Ancient

The configuration *'Atik* is superior to all the *Partsufim*.

פנימיות

Pnimiut

Internality

What is inside or interior. Also applies to deeper meaning or spirituality.

פרצוף

Partsuf

Configuration - Countenance

A *Partsuf* is a configuration of one or more *Sephirot* acting in coordination.

פרצופים

Partsufim

Configurations

See Partsuf

צדיק

Tsadik

Righteous

State of outmost closeness to the *Kedushah* and distance from the *Sitra A'hra (negative force)*. Also attributed to the *Sephira Yesod*.

צינור

Tsinor

Conduit

A *Sephira* is, in a way, a "conduit" that transforms the light into a particular force or quality, by which the Creator guides the worlds.

צל"ם

Tselem

Mo'hin (brains) of Z'A

The *Tselem* are the directive force - *Mo'hin* (brains) given to Z'A.

צמצום

Tsimtsum

Contraction – Retraction

The "*Tsimtsum*" is the first act of the *Ein Sof* (Infinite) in the creation. It is the retraction of His light from a certain space and encircling it, so as to reduce its intensity and allow created beings to exist.

קבלה

Kabbalah

The Kabbalah is the mystical and esoteric explanation of the

Torah. It teaches the unfolding of the worlds, the various ways of guidance of these worlds, the role of man in the creation, the will of the Creator and so on. It comprises of numerous other sciences as: astrology, cosmology, *Gematria*, metaphysics, demonology, physiognomy, palmistry, healing, alchemy, reincarnation, exorcism, prophecy etc.

קבלה מעשית

Kabbalah Ma'asit

Practical Kabbalah

The "other" type of Kabbalah, where names or combinations of names of angels are used with special signs or incantations, to invoke particular powers and alter normal states of events.

קדוש

Kadosh

Holly – Saintly

State of closeness to the *Kedushah* and distance from the *Sitra A'hra* (negative force).

קדוש ברוך הוא

Kadosh Barukh Hu

Saintly and Blessed He is

One of the names of G-od.

קדושה

Kedushah

Sanctity – Holiness

By accomplishing the *Mitsvot* and by the prayers, men do the *Tikunim* (rectifications) necessary to detach the *Klipot* from the *Kedushah.* The ultimate goal is to create a maximum distance from the negative force, and closeness to the *Kedushah.*

קו
Kav
Ray – Line
Ray of light that emerged from the *Ein Sof* (infinite) and entered on one side of the vacant space after the *Tsimtsum*.

קודשא בריך הוא
Kudsha Berikh Hu
Saintly and Blessed He is

קליפות
Klipot
Husks (negative forces)
The *Klipot* are the manifestation of the negative force.

קלקול
Kilkul
Deterioration – Damage
Kilkul is the opposite of *Tikun* (rectification).

קמיע
Kmi'a
Amulet
Names, or combinations of names of angels, with special signs, written on parchment to protect or to invoke particular powers.

רוח
Rua'h
Soul - Second level of the soul
Rua'h is the second level and is acquired before the next levels.

רוחני
Ru'hani
Spiritual
A spiritual person will give importance to the higher meaning of things, and live in the path of rightness to strengthen himself constantly.

רחל
Ra'hel
Ra'hel - configuration Nukvah
Configuration *Ra'hel* is of the aspect of kindness.

רמח"ל
Ramhal
Initials of Rabbi Moshe 'Haim Luzzatto

רע
Ra'
Evil – Bad
See Sitra A'hra

רפ"ח נצוצות
Rapa'h Nitsutsot
288 sparks
See Nitsutsot

רצון להשפיע
Ratson Lehashpia'
Will to bestow
The will of the Creator is to bestow goodness on His creatures.

רצון לקבל
Ratson Lekabel
Desire to receive
By his nature, man is himself a *Keli* (recipient) with a will to receive without limits.

רשימו
Reshimu
Imprint – trace
Imprint of the first light that remained inside. Everything is contained in potentiality in this imprint. Nothing could come to existence without having its origin in it.

שבירת הכלים
Shvirat HaKelim
Breaking of the vessels
Important damage caused by the seven lower *Sephirot* that could not hold the influx of their lights and subsequently broke.

שבת
Shabbat
The seventh day, *Shabbat* corresponds to the seventh *Sephira Malkhut*.

שורש
Shoresh
Root
Everything in existence has its root in the upper realms.

שכינה
Shekhina
Divine presence
One of the names of G-od.

שכר
Sakhar
Reward
The variable guidance is on the basis of justice, reward and punishment and is dependant on the actions of man. This guidance is by the linear *Sephirot*.

שער
Sha'ar
Gate – Portal
Entrance to a dimension. Gate to enter a knowledge.

תא חזא
Ta 'Haze
Come see (pay attention)
Expression frequently used in the *Zohar*.

תורה
Torah
The Kabbalah is the mystical and esoteric explanation of the Torah. All the profound secrets explained in the Kabbalah, are alluded to in the letters, words and different stories narrated in the Torah.

תחית המתים
T'hiyat ha Metim
Resurrection of the dead
Final goal of the six thousand years.

תיקון
Tikun
Rectification or action
In Hebrew, the word *"Tikun"* has different meanings. It can be understood as reparation or rectification but also as function, relation or action.

תפארת
Tiferet
Sephira (beauty)
Sixth of the *Sephirot*.

תפילה
Tefilah
Prayer
The order of the prayers is based on the systems of ascension of the worlds, as explained in the Kabbalah. The purpose of this ascension of the worlds is to provoke a union between the masculine and feminine configurations of each world, that they might bestow positive energies as a result of this harmony. At this level of comprehension, we understand that our prayers have a direct influence on the superior worlds, and on their guidance.

תפילות
Tefilot
Prayers

תרי"ג
Taryag
613

There are 613 veins and bones in man. Similarly, there are 613 *Mitsvot*, 613 parts to the soul, and 613 lights in each *Sephira* or configuration. This number is not arbitrary, as there are important interrelations and interactions between them.

ACRONYMS

Very often we find in the Zohar and in most Kabbalah texts acronyms, which are the initials or abbreviations of words or concepts. There are two main reasons why the acronyms are used, first, to avoid rewriting the same words again and again, and the second more important reason is to keep away the non initiated learner.

Acromym		L	Word - s
א"א	A"A	A	**Arikh Anpin** *Partsuf Arikh Anpin*
א"א	A"A	H	**Abraham Avinu** Our Father Abraham
א"א	A"A	H	**I Efshar** Impossible
א"ד	A"D	H	**Aino Dome** Does not resemble
א"י	E"I	H	**Erets Israel** Land of Israel
א"ס	E"S	H	**Ein Sof,** The without end or limit
א"פ	A"P	H	**A'Hor Be Panim** Back to front
א"צ	A"TS	H	**Aino Tsarikh** Not necessary
א"ק	A"K	A	**Adam Kadmon** Primordial man
א"ר	A"R	A	**Amar Rav** Rav said

227

KABBALAH CONCEPTS

Acromym		L	Word - s
אב"א	A"A	H	***A'hor Be A'hor*** Back to back
אבי"ע	ABYA	H	***Atsilut, Beriah, Yetsirah and Asiah***
אדה"ר	ADH"R	H	**Adam ha Rishon** The first man
אה"ל	AH"L	H	***Or Halevanah*** Light of the moon
או"א	Av"I	H	***Abah ve Imah*** *Partsufim Abah* and *Imah*
או"ח	O'"H	H	***Or 'Hozer*** Returning light
או"י	O"Y	H	***Or Yosher*** Straight light
או"מ	O"M	H	***Or Makif*** Encircling light
או"פ	O"P	H	***Or Pnimi*** Interior light
אח"פ	O'H"P	H	***Ozen, 'Hotem, Pey*** Ear, nose, mouth

ACRONYMS

Acromym		L	Word - s
אי'	IY'	H	**Imah** Partsuf Imah
אמ"ר	AM"R	H	**Or, Mayim, Rakia'** Light, Water, Firmament
אע"ג	A' "G	A	**Af 'al Gav** Even then
אע"פ	A' " P	H	**Af 'al Pi** Even so
אצ"ל	ATS"L	H	**Ain Tsarikh Lomar** Not necessary to mention
אתב"ש	ATB"SH	H	**ATBASH** Permutation of the letters
אתעד"ל	AT'D"L	A	**It'urerut Del'ela** Awakening from above
אתעד"ת	AT'D"T	A	**It'urerut DelTata** Awakening from lower
ב"ן	BaN (52)	H	**BaN** (52) Miluy of the name with a total of 52
ב"פ	B"P	A	**Shte Pe'amim** Two times

KABBALAH CONCEPTS

Acromym		L	Word - s
באד"ר	BAD"R	A	**Be Adra Raba** In the book of *Adra Raba* (Zohar)
באדר"ז	BADR"Z	A	**Be Adra Zouta** In the book of *Adra Zouta* (Zohar)
בג"ה	BG"H	H	**Binah, Gevurah, Hod** *Sephirot, left pillar*
בחי"	B'HY	H	**Be'hina** Quality – Attribute
בי"ע	BYA	H	**Beriah, Yetsirah, Asiah** Worlds
ביהמ"ק	BYHM"K	H	**Beit ha Mikdash** Temple
בכ"מ	BC"M	H	**Becol Makom** All the time – Everywhere
בכ"מ	BC"M	H	**Bekama Mekomot** Often – In a few places
במ"א	BM"A	H	**Bemakon Aher** In another place
במ"ר	BM"R	H	**Bemidrash Rabah** In the *Midrash Rabah*

230

ACRONYMS

Acromym		L	Word - s
בס"ד	BS"D	A	**Besa'ita deshmaya** With heaven's help
בסו"ה	BSU"H	H	**Besod Hakatuv** In the secret meaning
בע"ה	B'"A	H	**Be'ezrat Hashem** With the help of G-od
בע"ת	B' "T	H	**Ba'al Teshuva** One who makes *Teshuva*
בעה"ח	B' H" 'H	H	**Be'Ets Ha'haim** In the (book of) *'Ets Ha'haim*
בעוה"ב	B'OH"B	H	**Be'Olam Haba** In the future world
בעוה"ז	B'OH"Z	H	**Be'Olam Haze** In this world
בר"ת	BR"T	H	**Berashe Tevot** *In the initials*
בת"ת	BT"T	H	**BeTiferet** In the *(Sephira) Tiferet*
ג' גו ג'	G' go G'	H	**Shalosh Beshalosh** Three on three
ג"א	G"A	H	**Shalosh Etsma'iot**

231

Acromym	L	Word - s
		The three middle ones
ג"ט קר"ע פ"ח	G"T KR" ' P" 'H	A	**Gulgota, Tela, Kerumah, Ra'ava, 'Emer, Peki'hu, 'Hotma** Seven *Tikunim* of the head of *Arikh Anpin*
ג"כ	G"C	H	**Gam ken** Also
ג"ע	G" '	H	**Gan 'Eden** Garden of *Eden*
ג"ר	G"aR	H	**The three first Sephirot** *Keter, 'Hokhma, Binah. Or, 'Hokhma, Binah, Da'at.*
ג"ת	G"T	H	**Shalosh Ta'htonot** The three lower ones
גי'	GY'	H	**Gematria** Total of the letters
דו"ן	D"uN	A	**Dukhrin VeNukvin** Masculine and feminine
דצח"מ	DaTzHaM	H	**Domem, Tsomea'h, 'Hay, Medaber**

ACRONYMS

Acromym		L	Word - s
			Mineral, vegetal, animal and the spoken
ד"א	D"A	H	**Derekh A'her** An other way
ד"א	D"A	H	**Davar A'her** Something else
דת"י	DT"Y	H	**Da'at, Tiferet, Yesod** *Sephirot,* middle pillar
ה"ג	H"G	H	**'Hamesh Gevurot** Five *Gevurot*
ה"ח	H" 'H	H	**'Hamesh 'Hasadim** *Five 'Hasadim*
ה"ס	H"S	A	**He Sod** It is the secret
ה"פ	H"P	H	**'Hamesh Partsufim** Five *Partsufim*
ה"ר	H"R	H	**'Hamesh Rishonot** Five first ones
ה"ת	H"T	H	**'Hamesh Ta'htonot** Five lower ones
הנ"ל	HN"L	H	**Hanizcar Le'il**

233

Acromym		L	Word - s
			As mentioned above
הק'	HK'	H	**HaKadosh** The Saintly
הקב"ה	HKB"H	H	**HaKadosh Barukh Hu** Saintly and Blessed He is
השי"ת	HSHY"T	H	**HaShem Itbarakh** G-od may He be blessed
ו"ק	V"K	H	**Shesh Ketsavot** Six edges
ו"ת	V"T	H	**Shesh Ta'htonot** Six lower ones
וד"ל	VD"L	H	**Veday Lemavin** It is enough for the one who understands
והמ"י	VHM"Y	H	**Vehamaskil Yavin** And the wise will understand
והמ"י	VHM"Y	H	**VeHamaskil Yavin** And the wise will understand
וזה"ד	VZH"D	H	**Ve ze HaDin** And this is the law

Acromym		L	Word - s
וכו'	VCU'	H	**Vekhule** And so on
ועד"ז	V'D"Z	H	**Ve'al Derekh Ze** And in this way
ועכ"ז	V'C"Z	H	**Ve'im kol Ze** And with all this
ותי'	VTY'	H	**VeTikunim** And the *Tikunim*
ז"א	Z"A	A	**Zeir Anpin** *Partsuf*
ז"ח	Z"T	H	**Zain Ta'htonot** Seven lower ones
ז"ח	Z" 'H	H	**Zohar 'Hadash** Part of the *Zohar*
ז"ל	Z"L	H	**Zikhrono Lebrakha** His remembrance is blessed
ז"ל	Z"L	H	**Ze Leshono** This is his words (quotation)
ז"מ	Z"M	A	**Shiv'ha Malkin** Seven kings

Acromym		L	Word - s
ז"ס	Z"S	H	**Ze Sod** This is the secret
ז"ע	Z" '	H	**Ze 'Enian** This Subject
ז"ת	Za"T	1	**Zain Ta'htonot** Seven lower *Sephirot*
זא"ז	ZA"Z	H	**Ze Etsel Ze** This one in this one
זו"ן	Z"Un	A	**Zeir Anpin and Nukvah** *Partsufim*
זל"ז	ZL"Z	H	**Ze la Ze** This one to this one
זמ"ז	ZM"Z	H	**Ze mi Ze** This one from this one
זמ"ן נק"ט	ZM"N NK"T	H	**Zera'im, Mo'hed, Nashim,** **Nezikim, Kadashim, Tehorot** Six orders of *Mishna – Guemara*
זע"ז	Z' "Z	H	**Ze 'al Ze** This one on this one
ח"א	'H"A	H	**'Helek Rishon** First part

ACRONYMS

Acromym		L	Word - s
ח"ב	'H"B	H	**'Helek Sheni** Second part
ח"ו	'H"V	H	**'Has Veshalom** G-od Forbid
ח"ס	'H"S	A	**'Hokhma Stimaah** *Sephira*
חב"ד	'HBD	H	**'Hokhma, Binah and Da'at** *Sephirot*
חג"ת	'HGT	H	**Hesed, Gevurah and Tiferet** *Sephirot*
חד"ר	'HD"R	H	**'Hesed, Din, Ra'hamim** Bounty, rigor and mercy
חו"ב	'HV"B	H	**'Hokhma VeBinah** *Sephirot*
חו"ג	'HV"G	H	**'Hesed VeGevurah** *Sephirot*
חו"ג	'HV"G	H	**'Hasadim VeGevurot** Qualities
חו"ל	'HU"L	H	**'Huts LaAretz** Outside Erets Israel

237

Acromym		L	Word - s

חז"ל   'HZ"L   H   ***'Hokhmanu Z'aL***
Our *sages* of blessed memory

חח"ן   'H'H"N   H   ***'Hokhma, 'Hesed, Netsa'h***
Sephirot, right pillar

חל"ה   'HL"H   H   ***'Helek Le'Olam Haba***
A part for the world to come

חע"ה   'H""H   H   ***'Haye 'Olam Haba***
Life in the world to come

ט"ס   T"S   H   ***Tesha' Sephirot***
Nine *Sephirot*

ט"ר   T"R   H   ***Tesha' Rishonot***
Nine first *Sephirot*

ט"ת   T"T   H   ***Tesha' Ta'htonot***
Nine lower ones

טו"ר   TV"R   H   ***Tov veRa'***
Good and bad

טנת"א   TaNTA   H   ***Ta'amim, Nekudot, Tagin,* and**
Autiot.
Cantillation, vowels, crowns and
letters

י"א   Y"A   H   ***Yesh Oserim***
Some forbid

Acromym	L	Word - s
א"י Y"A	H	**Yesh Omerim** Some say
מ"י Y"M	H	**Yesh Mekomot** In some places
מ"י Y"M	H	**Yesh Mefareshim** Some explain
ס"י Y"S	H	**'Assarah Sephirot** Ten *Sephirot*
יה"א YH"A	H	**Yud, He, Aleph** The three *Miluyim* of the *Tetragamon*
יו"ש YV"SH	H	**Yamin Usmall** Right and left
יחנר"ו Y'HNR"V	H	**Ye'hidah, 'Hayah, Neshama, Rua'h, Nefesh** Five level of the soul
יט"ל YT"L	H	**Yesh Ta'ham Ledavar** There is a reason for this saying
יוי" YY"Y	H	**Yud, Yud, Yud** *Yebarekhekha, Yaer, Yisa* (Three first words of the *Birkat Kohanim*)

Acromym		L	Word - s
יסו"ת	ISOT	A	**Israel Saba and Tevunah** *Partsufim*
יצ"ט	YTS"T	H	**Yetser Tov** Good instinct
יצה"ר	YTSH"R	H	**Yetser Hara'** Bad instinct
יש"א	YS"A	H	**Yamin, Small, Emtsa'h** Right, left, middle
ישסו"ת	ISOT	A	**Israel Saba and Tevunah** *Partsufim*
ישסו"ת ב	ISOT 2	1	**Israel Saba and Tevunah 2** *Partsufim*
כ"א	C"A	H	**Kakh Amar** This way it is said
כ"א	C"A	H	**Kol E'had** Each one
כ"ב	C"B	H	**22** Twenty two letters
כ"ג	C"G	H	**Kohen Gadol** High priest

Acromym		L	Word - s
כ"ה	C"H	A	**Katuv Hakha** Written this way
כ"ז	C"Z	H	**Kol Zman** All the time
כ"ז	C"Z	H	**Kol Ze** All this
כ"ח	C" 'H	H	**Keli 'Hitson** Middle *Keli*
כ"י	C"Y	H	**Knesset Israel** Assembly of Israel
כ"כ	C"C	H	**Kol Kakh** So much
כ"מ	C"M	A	**Kan Mashma'** This way we understand
כ"מ	C"M	H	**Kan Matsati** This way I found
כ"מ	C"M	H	**Kol Makom** In every place – All the time
כ"ע	C" '	H	**Keter 'Elyon** Upper *Keter*

Acromym		L	Word - s
כ"פ	C"P	H	***Keli Pnimi*** Interior *Keli*
כאו"א	CAV"A	H	***Kol E'had veE'had*** Each and everyone
כה"א	CH"A	H	***Kakh Hu Omer*** As he says
כח"ב	*K'HB*	H	***Keter, 'Hokhma, Binah*** *Sephirot*
כחב"ד	K'HB"D	H	***Keter, 'Hokhma, Binah, Da'at*** *Sephirot*
כל"י	CL"Y	H	***Kohen, Levi, Israel*** Three types of Bne Israel
כמו"ש	CMV"SH	H	***Kemo Shekatuv*** As it is written
כנ"ל	CN"L	H	***Kenizcar Le'il*** As mentioned above
כנז'	CNZ'	H	***Kenizcar*** As mentioned
כצ"ל	CTS"L	H	***Ken Tsarikh Lomar*** It should be said this way

ACRONYMS

Acromym		L	Word - s
כש"ש	CSH"SH	H	**Kemo Shekatavti Sham** As I have written there
ל"ג	L"G	H	**Lashon Guemara** In the language of the Guemara
ל"ז	L"Z	H	**Lashon Zakhar** Masculine designation
ל"כ	L"C	H	**Lo Katuv** It is not written
ל"כ	L"C	H	**Lo Khen** Not this way
ל"נ	L"N	H	**Lashon Nekevah** Feminine designation
ל"נ	L"N	H	**Li Nirey** In my opinion
ל"צ	L"TS	H	**Lo Tsarikh** Not necessary
ל"ת	L"T	H	**Lo Ta'asse** Not to do
לבנ"ה	LVN"H	H	**LaV Netivot Ha'Hokhma** 32 Paths of wisdom

Acromym		L	Word - s
לד"א	LD"A	H	**LeDavar A'her** Something else
לד"א	LD"A	H	**LeDa'at A'herim** In the opinion of others
לד"ה	LD"H	H	**LeDivre Hakol** In the opinion of all
לכ"ע	LC" '	A	**Lekule 'Alma** All the time
למה"ד	LMH"D	H	**Lema Hadavar Domey** To what does this resemble
לעת"ל	L'T"L	H	**Le'atid Lavo** In the future
לש"ש	LSH"SH	H	**Leshem Shamaim** With no personal interest
מ"א	M"A	H	**Minhag Avoteynu** Our father's custom
מ"ב	M"B	H	**Forty two** Name of forty two letters
מ"ד	M"D	A	**Mayin Dukhrin** Masculine waters

Acromym		L	Word - s
מ"ה	M"H	H	**MaH** (45) Miluy of the name with a total of 52
מ"מ	M"M	H	**Mikol Makon** Anyways
מ"ן	M"N	A	**Mayin Nukvin** Feminine waters
מ"ע	M" '	H	**Mitsvot 'Assey** Positive commandments
מ"ש	M"SH	H	**Ma Shekatuv** What is written
מב"ד	MB"D	H	**Moshia'h ben David** *Messia'h* son of David
מדה"ד	MDH"D	H	**Midat HaDin** Attribute of rigor
מדה"נ	MDH"N	H	**Midrash HaNe'elam** *Midrash*
מדה"ר	MDH"R	H	**Midat HaRa'hamim** Attribute of mercy
מה"מ	MH"M	H	**Malakh Hamavet** Angel of death

Acromym		L	Word - s
מה"ש	MH"SH	H	**Malakhe Hasharet** Ministering Angels
מו"מ	MU"M	H	**Ma'alah UMatah** Above and under
מו"ס	Mo"S	A	**Mo'ha Stimaa** *Sephira*
מט"ט	MT"T	H	**Matatro-n** Name of one of the main angels
מכ"ש	MC"SH	H	**Mikol Sheken** Moreover
מל'	ML'	A	**Malkhut** *Sephira*
מל"ת	ML"T	H	**Mitsva Lo Ta'asey** Negative commandment
מנצפ"ך	MNTSP"KH	H	**Five ending letters** Five *Gevurot*
מע"ט	M'"T	H	**Ma'asim Tovim** Good deeds
מרע"ה	MR' "H	H	**Moshe Rabenu 'Alav Hashalom** Moshe *Rabenu*, peace on him

Acromym		L	Word - s
מרשב"י	MRSHB"Y	A	**Meamre Rabbi Shim'on Bar Yo'hai** Saying of Rabbi Shim'on Bar Yo'hai
משא"כ	MSHA"C	H	**MaH Sheen Ken** Which is not
נ"ר	N"R	H	**Nefesh, Rua'h** Soul
נה"י	NHY	H	**Netsa'h, Hod and Yesod** *Sephirot*
נהי"ם	NHY"M	H	**Netsa'h, Hod, Yesod, Malkhut** *Sephirot*
נו"ה	NV"H	H	**Netsa'h veHod** *Sephirot*
נוק'	NUK'	A	**Nukvah** *Partsuf* - Feminine
ני"ק	NY"K	A	**Nitsusot Kadishin** Holy sparks
נל"נ	NL"N	H	**Neshama le Neshama** Higher level of the *Neshama*
נק'	NK'	H	**Nikra** Called

Acromym		L	Word - s
נר"ן	NaRaN	H	**Nefesh, Rua'h, Neshama** Levels of the souls
נרנח"י	NRNHY	H	**Nefesh, Rua'h, Neshama,' Hayah and Ye'hidah** Levels of the souls
נש"ב	NSH"B	H	**Nun Sha'are Binah** 50 paths of understanding
נת"א	NT"A	H	**Nekudot, Tagin, Autiot** Vowel, crowns and letters
ס"א	S"A	A	**Sitra A'hra** Negative side
ס"א	S"A	H	**Sefarim A'herim** Other books
ס"א	S"A	A	**Sitrey Autiot** Secret of the letters
ס"ג	S"G	H	**SaG** Miluy of the name with a total of 63
ס"מ	S"M	H	**Sam...l** Name of the main destructive Angel

ACRONYMS

Acromym		L	Word - s
ת"ס	S"T	H	**Sofe Tevot** Ending letters
ת"ס	S"T	A	**Sitrey Torah** Secrets of the Torah
ה"וס	SO"H	H	**Sod Hakatuv** The secret in the writing
י"פס	SP"Y	A	**Sephira**
א"ע	'A"A	H	**'Anaf Rishon** First branch
א"ע	'A"A	H	**'Amud Aleph** First paragraph or page
ב"ע	'A"B	H	**'A"V** Miluy of the name with a total of 72
ד"ע	'A"D	H	**'Al Derekh** In this way
ה"ע	'A"H	H	**'Alav HaShalom** Peace on him
ה"ע	'A"H	H	**'Asarat Devarim** The ten sayings (of creation)

Acromym		L	Word - s
ע"ה	'A"H	H	*'Am HaArets* Ignorant man
ע"ה	'E"H	H	*'Ein Hara'* Evil eye
ע"ה	'E"H	H	*'Eved HaShem* G-od's servant
ע"הר	'E"HR	H	*'Ein Hara'* Evil eye
ע"ז	'A"Z	H	*'Al ze* On this
ע"ז	'A"Z	H	*'Avodah Zarah* Idolatry
ע"ח	'E" 'H	H	*'Ets 'Haim* Tree of life
ע"י	'A"Y	A	*'Atik Yomin* Partsuf
ע"כ	'A"C	H	*'Al ken* Therefore
ע"כ	'A"C	H	*'Avodat Kokhavim* Idolatry

Acromym		L	Word - s
ע"כ	'A"C	H	**'Ad kan** Until here
ע"ל	'A"L	H	**'Ayn Le'il** Explained above
ע"מ	'A"M	H	**'Al Menat** In order of
ע"ס	'E"S	H	**'Eser Sephirot** Ten *Sephirot*
ע"פ	'A"P	H	**'Al Pi** Therefore
ע"ק	'A"K	A	**'Atika Kadisha** *Partsuf*
ע"ש	'A"SH	H	**'Ayin Sham** Explained there
עד"ה	'AD"H	H	**'Al Derekh Hakatuv** As it is written
עד"מ	'AD"M	H	**'Al Derekh Mashal** As in a parable
עה"ד	'AH"D	H	**'Ets Hada'at** Tree of knowledge

Acromym		L	Word - s
עו"נ	''A"V"N	A	**'Atik VeNukve** 'Atid and his Nukvah
עוה"ז	'OVH"Z	H	**'Olam Haze** This world
עי"ז	'AY"Z	H	**'Al Yede ze** Since – Therefore
עי"מ	'Y"M	H	**'Ibur, Yenikah, Mo'hin** Gestation, Suckling, Mo'hin
עיה"ק	'YH"K	H	**'Ir HaKodesh** Holy city
עכ"ד	'AC"D	H	**'Ad Kan Debarav** Until here his words (end of quotation)
עכ"ל	'AC"L	H	**'Ad Kan Leshono** Until here his words (end of quotation)
עכ"פ	'AC"P	H	**'Al Kol Panim** Anyways
עכו"מ	'ACU"M	H	**'Oved Kokhavim VeMazalot** Idolater
עסמ"ב	'ASM"B	H	**'A"V, SaG, MaH, BaN** Four spellings of the Name

252

ACRONYMS

Acromym		L	Word - s
			YKVK
עצה"ד	'ETSH"D	H	***'Ets Hada'at*** Tree of Knowledge
עש"ה	'ASH"H	H	***'Ayin Sham Etev*** Better explained there
פ"	PY'	H	***Pirush*** Explanation
פ"א	P"A	H	***Perek Rishon*** First paragraph
פב"א	PB"A	H	***Panim B A'hor*** Face to Back
פב"פ	PB"P	H	***Panin B Panim*** Face to Face
פו"ח	PV" 'H	H	***Penimiut ve'Hitsoniut*** Interiority and exteriority
פלחה"ק	PL'HH"K	H	***Peti'ha Le'hokhma HaKabbalah*** Introduction to the knowledge of Kabbalah
פרד"ס	PRD"S	H	***Pshat, Remez, Drash, Sod*** Literal, Allusion, Homiletic, Secret

253

Acromym		L	Word - s
צ"ע	TS" 'I	H	***Tsarikh 'Iyun*** Needs to be explained
צח"מ	TH'H"M	H	***Tsomea'h, 'Hay, Medaber*** Vegetal, Animal, Spoken
ק"ק	K"K	H	***Kodshe Kodashim*** Holy of Holies
ק"ש	K"SH	H	***Keriat Shema'*** Reading of the *Shema'*
קב"ח	KB"H	A	***Kudsha Berikh Hu*** Saintly and blessed He is
קבו"ש	KBH"SH	A	***Kudsha Berikh Hu VeShkhinte*** Saintly and blessed He is and His *Shekhina*
קוש"י	KUSH"Y	H	***Kutsu shel Yud*** The edge (top part) of the letter *Yud*
קל"י	KLY'	H	***Klipot*** Husks
קמ"ג	*KM"G*		***KM"G*** *Miluy* of the name א-ה-י-ה With the letter א

Acromym		L	Word - s
קנ"א	KN"A		**KN"A** *Miluy* of the name א-ה-י-ה With the letter ה
קס"א	KS"A		**KS"A** *Miluy* of the name א-ה-י-ה With the letter י
ר"א	R"A	H	***Rabbi Aba*** One of the main figures of the *Zohar*
ר"א	R"A	H	***Rabbi El'azar*** Son of Rabbi Shim'on Bar Yo'hay
ר"חו	R'HV	H	***Rabbi Haim Vital*** Main student of the Ari Z'al
ר"י	R"Y	H	***Rabbi Yehudah*** One of the main figures of the *Zohar*
ר"י	R"Y	H	***Rabbi Yossi*** One of the main figures of the *Zohar*
ר"י	R"Y	H	***Rabbi Its'hak*** One of the main figures of the *Zohar*

Acromym		L	Word - s
ר"ל	R"L	H	**Retsono Lomar** He wants, or means to say
רדל"א	Rdl'a	H	**Radl"a** The Unknown Head
רה"י	RH"Y	H	**Reshut Haya'hid** Private property
רה"ק	RH"K	H	**Rua'h HaKodesh** Divine inspiration
רה"ר	RH"R	H	**Reshut HaRabim** Public property
רמ"ק	RM"K	H	**Rabbi Moshe Kordovero** *Kabbalist* of *Tsfat*
רמח"ל	RM'H"L	H	**Rabbi Moshe Haim Luzzatto** *Kabbalist* from *Padova Italy*
רע"צ	R'l'm	A	**Ra'ia Mehimana** Part of the *Zohar*
רפ"ח	RP" 'H	H	**Rapa'h** 288 (*Netsutsot*)
רשב"י	RSHB"Y	H	**Rabbi Shim'on Bar Yo'hay** Author of the *Zohar*

ACRONYMS

Acromym		L	Word - s
רשר"ד	RSHR"D	H	**Reiya, Shemi'ah, Reya'h, Dibur** Sight, hearing, smell and speech
ש'	SH"	H	**Sha'ar** Entrance (book, chapter)
ש"א	SH"A	H	**Shelish Emtsa'i** Middle third
ש"א	SH"A	H	**Shelish Rishon** First third
ש"ב	SH"B	H	**Shelish Sheni** Second third
ש"ע	SH" '	H	**Shelish 'Elyon** Higher third
ש"ת	SH"T	H	**Shelish Ta'hton** Lower third
שביה"כ	SHBYH"C	H	**Shvirat HaKelim** Breaking of the vessels
שנא"ן	SHNA"N	H	**Shor, Aryeh, Nesher, Adam** Four faces of the *Merkavah*
שס"ה	SHS"H	H	**365** Number

Acromym		L	Word - s
ת"ד	T"D	A	**Tikuna Dikna** *Tikunim* of the *Dikna*
ת"ז	T"Z	H	**Tikune Zohar** Part of the *Zohar*
ת"ח	T" 'H	A	**Ta 'Haze** Come see
ת"ח	T" 'H	H	**Talmid 'Hakham** Knowledgeable man
ת"ח	T" 'H	H	**Tikunim 'Hadashim** Part of the *Zohar*
ת"ש	T"SH	A	**Ta Shema'** Listen
ת"ת	T"T	H	**Tiferet** *Sephira*
תו"מ	TV"M	H	**Tiferet, Malkhut** *Sephirot*
תושב"ב	TSHB"C	H	**Torah SheBikhtav** Written Torah
תושב"פ	TSHB"P	H	**Torah SheBe'alpe** Oral Torah

Acromym	L	Word - s
תכ"ת	TC"T	A	***Telat Klalin BeTelat*** Three on three
תרי"ג	TRY"G	H	***613*** Number
תש"י	TSH"Y	H	***Tefilin shel Yad*** *Tefilin* of the hand
תש"ר	TSH"R	H	***Tefilln shel Rosh*** *Tefilin* of the head

Bibliography

From the Ram'hal

כללות האילן הקדוש
פתחי חכמה ודעת
קלח פתחי חכמה
כללים ראשונים
אדיר במרום

From the Ari Z'al

כתבי הארי
עץ חיים
שער רוח הקודש
שער הגלגולים

ספר הזהר
The Zohar
Rabbi Shim'on Bar Yo'hai

The Kabbalah of the Ari Z'al, according to the Ramhal
Rabbi Raphael Afilalo, Kabbalah Editions

Kabbalah Dictionary and Kabbalah Glossary
Rabbi Raphael Afilalo, Kabbalah Editions

דרך חכמת האמת לרמחל
Rav Mordekhai Chriqui, Editions Ramhal, Jerusalem

האילן הקדוש לרמחל
Rav Shalom Oulman (Jerusalem)

Index

TABLES

Soul	World
Ye'hidah	Atsilut
'Hayah	Atsilut
Neshama	Beriah
Rua'h	Yetsirah
Nefesh	'Asiah

Soul	Configuration
Ye'hidah	Arikh Anpin
'Hayah	Abah
Neshama	Imah
Rua'h	Zeir Anpin
Nefesh	Nukvah

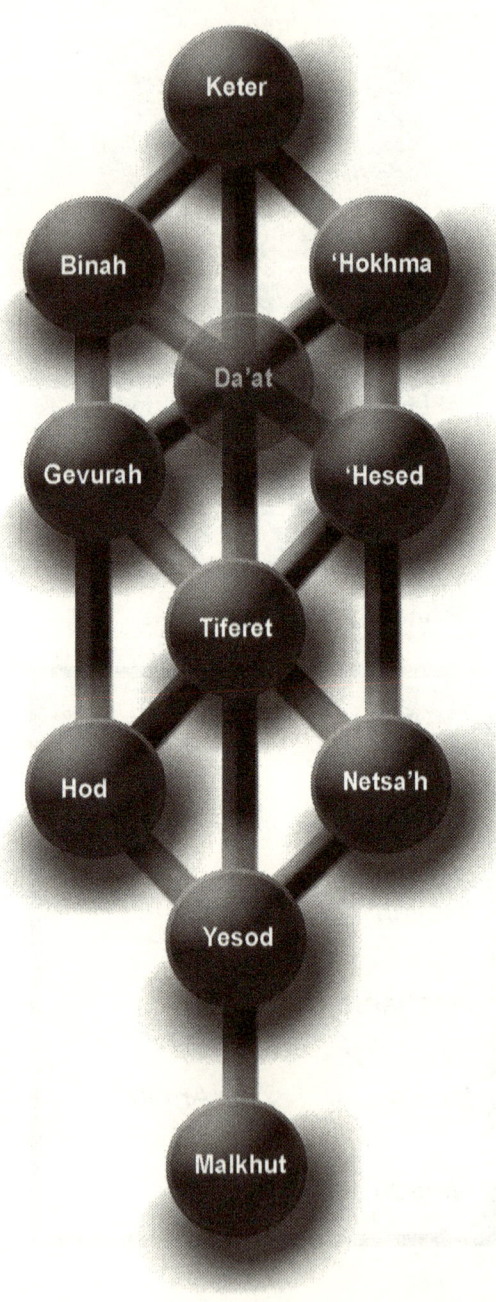

Sephira		Column	Position
Keter	Crown	Mercy	Center
'Hokhma	Wisdom	Kindness	Right
Binah	Understanding	Rigor	Left
Da'at	Knowledge	Mercy	Center
'Hesed	Bounty	Kindness	Right
Gevurah	Rigor	Rigor	Left
Tiferet	Beauty	Mercy	Center
Netsa'h	Glory	Kindness	Right
Hod	Splendor	Rigor	Left
Yesod	Foundation	Mercy	Center
Malkhut	Kingship	Mercy	Center

Sephira	Metal	Direction
'Hesed	Silver	South
Gevurah	Gold	North
Tiferet	Copper	East
Netsa'h	Tin	Above
Hod	Lead	Lower
Yesod	Silver	West
Malkhut	Iron	Center

Sephira	Level of the soul	Partsuf
Keter	Ye'hidah	'Atik Yomin Arikh Anpin
'Hokhma	Hayah	Abah Israel Saba
Binah	Neshama	Imah Tevunah
'Hesed	Rua'h	Zeir Anpin
Gevurah	Rua'h	Zeir Anpin
Tiferet	Rua'h	Zeir Anpin
Netsa'h	Rua'h	Zeir Anpin
Hod	Rua'h	Zeir Anpin
Yesod	Rua'h	Zeir Anpin
Malkhut	Nefesh	Nukvah

Sephira	Day
'Hesed	Sunday
Gevurah	Monday
Tiferet	Tuesday
Netsa'h	Wednesday
Hod	Thursday
Yesod	Friday
Malkhut	Shabbat

Sephira	Physical correspondence	Face
Keter	Head	Head
'Hokhma	Right brain	Right brain
Binah	Left brain	Left brain
'Hesed	Right arm	Right eye
Gevurah	Left arm	Right ear
Tiferet	Body	Right nostril
Netsa'h	Right leg	Left eye
Hod	Left leg	Left ear
Yesod	Masculine organ	Left nostril
Malkhut	Crown on the masculine organ	Mouth

Sephira	Tetragamon	
Keter	י	Extremity of Yud
'Hokhma	י	Yud
Binah	ה	First HeY
'Hesed	ו	Vav
Gevurah	ו	Vav
Tiferet	ו	Vav
Netsa'h	ו	Vav
Hod	ו	Vav
Yesod	ו	Vav
Malkhut	ה	Second HeY

Sephira	Quality
Keter	Complete kindness to all, even to the not deserving
'Hokhma	Kindness to all, even to the not deserving (but less than Keter, and not always)
Binah	Kindness to all, even to the less deserving (but from her, the rigors start)
Da'at	Guidance that makes the equilibrium between 'Hokhmah and Binah
'Hesed	Complete kindness to who is deserving
Gevurah	Full rigor to who is deserving
Tiferet	Kindness that makes the equilibrium between complete kindness and rigor
Netsa'h	Diminished kindness to who is deserving
Hod	Diminished rigor to who is deserving.
Yesod	Guidance that makes the equilibrium between Sephira Netsa'h and Hod
Malkhut	Guidance that translates all the superior emanations into one that is reflected to the creation Link or connection between all the superior Sephirot and man

לעלוי נשמת

Abraham David Hanania Afilalo bar Mira ז'ל

לעלוי נשמת

Salomon Afilalo ז'ל

Mira Afilalo ז'ל

לעלוי נשמת

Rav Abraham Chocron ז'ל

Gracia Chocron ז'ל

With the compliments of

Armand & Ria Afilalo

לעלוי נשמת

Rav Yeich Revah ז׳ל

Joseph Revah ז׳ל

Yacot Revah ז׳ל

Sylvie Revah ז׳ל

Israel Kakone ז׳ל

Simi Kakone ז׳ל

Mardoche Kakone ז׳ל

Salomon Kakone ז׳ל

לעלוי נשמת

Deborah Elbaz Bat Aziza ז׳ל

La'hziz Gozlan ז׳ל

Its'hak Chokron ז׳ל

Moshe Afilalo ז׳ל

Meyer Ohayon ז׳ל

David Ohnona ז׳ל

Richard Gabbay ז׳ל

Eliran Elbaz ben Yardena ז׳ל

David Haim Benyamin Knafo ז׳ל

With the compliments of

Marc & Marie-Elaine Afilalo

With the compliments of

Judah & Katy Bendayan

With the compliments of

Sonia & Scott C. Swchartz

www.ingramcontent.com/pod-product-compliance
Lightning Source LLC
Chambersburg PA
CBHW020438130626
46549CB00001B/205